THE SELLING
OF THE
PRESIDENT
1968

THE SELLING
OF THE
PRESIDENT

1968

by

Joe McGinniss

TRIDENT PRESS

NEW YORK

SBN: 671–27043–5

LIBRARY OF CONGRESS CATALOG CARD NUMBER: 77–92157
COPYRIGHT, ©, 1969, BY JOEMAC, INCORPORATED. ALL RIGHTS
RESERVED. NO PART OF THIS BOOK MAY BE REPRODUCED IN
ANY FORM WITHOUT PERMISSION IN WRITING FROM THE
PUBLISHER, EXCEPT BY A REVIEWER WHO MAY QUOTE
BRIEF PASSAGES IN A REVIEW TO BE PRINTED IN A
MAGAZINE OR NEWSPAPER.
PUBLISHED SIMULTANEOUSLY IN THE UNITED STATES AND
CANADA BY TRIDENT PRESS, A DIVISION OF SIMON & SCHUSTER,
INC., 630 FIFTH AVENUE, NEW YORK, N.Y. 10020
PRINTED IN THE UNITED STATES OF AMERICA

FOURTH PRINTING

For my parents, who care.

ACKNOWLEDGMENTS

I would like to thank some people who have helped me:

Warren Randall, of the *Port Chester Daily Item*
Paul Johnson, of the *Worcester Telegram*
Jack Wilson, of the *Philadelphia Bulletin*
John Gillen, of the *Philadelphia Inquirer*
Gene Prakapas, of Trident Press

"When style and charisma connotes the idea of contriving, of public relations, I don't buy it at all."

—Richard M. Nixon

"Our group used to get together often. Of course, none of us had much money at the time, so we would just meet at someone's house after skating and have food, a spaghetti dinner or something of that type, and then we would sit around and tell stories and laugh. Dick was always the highlight of the party because he has a wonderful sense of humor. He would keep everybody in stitches. Sometimes we would even act out parts. I will never forget one night when we did 'Beauty and the Beast.' Dick was the Beast, and one of the other men dressed up like Beauty. This sounds rather silly to be telling it now, but in those days we were all very young, and we had to do home entertainment rather than go out and spend money. We used to put on funny shows. It was all good, clean fun, and we had loads of laughs."

—Mrs. Richard M. Nixon

◄1►

Richard Nixon had taped a set of one- and five-minute commercials at the Hotel Pierre on Monday morning, October 21. Frank Shakespeare was not happy with the way they were done. "The candidate was harassed," he said. "Tired and harassed."

Shakespeare obtained backstage space at the theater on West Forty-fourth Street where the Merv Griffin Show was done, for Friday morning, October 25, and Richard Nixon agreed to do another set.

Mike Stanislavsky, an editor from Teletape, the film studio, was told to design a proper setting. He produced the usual: full bookcase, heavy brown desk—but with something new. A window. His design called for a window between the two bookcases behind the desk. "It adds lightness," he said. "Not just physically, but psychological lightness."

Harry Treleaven got to the theater at ten after ten Friday morning. The secret service already was there. The day was gray and cold, as so many recently had seemed to be. Treleaven walked to a table at the far end of the backstage area where paper cups were stacked next to a pot of coffee. At twenty minutes to eleven, the secret service received word: he's on his way.

Richard Nixon entered the studio at ten-fifty. He went

9

straight to an enclosed dressing room called the Green Room, where Ray Voege, the quiet, blond makeup man, was waiting with his powders and cloths.

Nixon came out of the Green Room at eleven o'clock. There was a drop of three or four inches from the doorway to the floor of the stage. He did not see it and stumbled as he stepped out the door. He grinned, reflexively, and Frank Shakespeare led him to the set.

He took his position on the front of the heavy brown desk. He liked to lean against a desk, or sit on the edge of one, while he taped commercials, because he felt this made him seem informal. There were about twenty people, technicians and advisers, gathered in a semicircle around the cameras.

Richard Nixon looked at them and frowned.

"Now when we start," he said, "don't have anybody who is not directly involved in this in my range of vision. So I don't go shifting my eyes."

"Yes, sir. All right, clear the stage. Everybody who's not actually doing something get off the stage, please. Get off the stage."

There was one man in a corner, taking pictures. His flash blinked several times in succession. Richard Nixon looked in his direction. The man had been hired by the Nixon staff to take informal pictures throughout the campaign, for historical purposes.

"Are they stills?" Richard Nixon said. "Are they our own stills? Well then, knock them off." He motioned with his arm. "Can them. We've got so goddamned many stills already."

Richard Nixon turned back toward the cameras.

"Now when you give me the fifteen-second cue, give it to me right under the camera. So I don't shift my eyes."

"Right, sir."

Then Len Garment came out with some figures about the

rising crime rate in Buffalo, which also happened to be an area where Nixon was falling far behind. It was felt at this time that the Buffalo margin for Humphrey could be large enough to cost Nixon New York State. Len Garment explained that they would like him to do a special one-minute commercial for Buffalo, concentrating on the rise in crime. He showed Nixon his papers with the statistics.

"Are the figures higher there?" Nixon said. Len Garment told him they were—significantly. Nixon studied the papers for a moment and then handed them back. "All right," he said.

Then they were ready to start. Richard Nixon sat at the edge of the desk, arms folded, eyes fixed on the camera lens.

"Now let me know just a second or so before you start," he said, "so you don't catch me frozen"—he made a face—"like this."

"Yes, sir. Okay, we're ready now."

"You're going to start now?"

"Right now, sir. Here we go." The red light on camera one began to glow, the camera made a low, whirring sound, and the tape machine emitted three beeps to indicate it was operating.

"As we enter the last few days of this critical campaign," Richard Nixon said, "one issue on which the greatest difference exists between the two candidates is that of law and order in the United States. Mr. Humphrey defends the record of the last four years. He defends the attorney general and his policies. I completely disagree with him in that respect. I say that when crime has been going up nine times as fast as population, when we've had riots in three hundred cities that have cost us two hundred dead and seven thousand injured, when forty-three percent of the American people are afraid to walk in the streets of their cities at night, then it's time for a complete housecleaning, it's time for a new attorney general, it's time to wage an all-out war against crime in the United States. I pledge that kind of activity. And I pledge to you that we will again have freedom from fear in the cities and in the streets of America."

He turned immediately to a technician.

"Let's try it once more," he said. "That was a little too long."

Frank Shakespeare said something from the side of the stage.

"Well, we won't use that one," Richard Nixon said. "Because I have another thought. I have to cut it just a little in the outset."

Frank Shakespeare said something else. The tape machine beeped three times.

"Yeah, I know, but we want to get another thought in at the last," Richard Nixon said.

Mike Stanislavsky stepped from behind a camera. "When you bring your head up and start talking, bring your head up and look at the camera for a moment . . ."

"Yeah." Richard Nixon nodded.

". . . and then start talking so that we can . . ."

"Okay, Mike?" a floor man asked.

Mike Stanislavsky turned. "Let's have quiet on the floor, please. There was a little noise during the last take. Stand by, please, here we go." He looked at Nixon. "When you're ready," he said.

"As we enter the last few days of this critical campaign," Richard Nixon said, "there's one issue on which the difference between the candidates is crystal clear. And that's the issue of law and order in the United States. Mr. Humphrey defends the record of the last four years, defends the attorney general and his policies." Nixon shook his head, to indicate disagreement. "I completely disagree with him," he said. "I say that when crime goes up nine times as fast as population, and when forty-three percent of the American people are afraid to walk on the streets of their cities at night, it's time for a complete housecleaning. I pledge a new attorney general. I pledge an—" He stumbled here as the pledges bumped one against the other in his mind.

"Oh, start again," he said. "Can you just keep it rolling?"

There were three beeps from the tape machine.

"Quiet, please, here we go," Mike Stanislavsky said. "When you're ready."

Al Scott and Harry Treleaven were watching from a control room one flight below the stage.

"I wish he'd use a teleprompter," Treleaven said.

"That's been bugging me for a year," Scott said. "People think he's reading anyway."

Nixon had refused the teleprompter from the start. He kept all the figures—crime rising nine times as fast . . . 300 cities . . . 200 dead . . . 7,000 injured . . . 43 percent of the American people afraid . . . He kept them all in his head, like the date of the Battle of Hastings.

Now he was starting again: "As we enter the last few days of the nineteen sixty-eight campaign, there is one issue on which there is a critical difference of opinion between the two candidates and that's on the issue of law and order in the United States. Mr. Humphrey pledges that he will continue the policies of the last—"

He stopped.

"I don't like that, either," he said. "Let's— We'll do another one here."

Again, three beeps from the machine. Richard Nixon sat at the edge of the desk, looking at the floor. He rested his chin on his fist.

"Thinking of the exact timing on this, and I'll get it right."
He paused, then nodded.

"All right," he said.

"Okay?" Mike Stanislavsky asked. "All right. Stand by.
Here we go again, please. Quiet."

"As we enter the last few days of this critical campaign of
nineteen sixty-eight, there is one issue on which there is a
complete difference of opinion between the two candidates.
That's the issue of law and order in the United States. Mr.
Humphrey defends the record of the last four years, he defends the attorney general and his policies. I completely disagree. I say that when we have had crime going up nine
times as fast as population, and when forty-three percent of
the American people are afraid to walk on the streets of their
cities at night, it's time for a new policy. I pledge a new attorney general. I pledge an all-out war against organized
crime in this country. I pledge that we shall have policies
that will restore freedom from fear on the streets of the cities
of America, and all over this great land of ours."

The cameras stopped.

"It's all right if it's a little short," Richard Nixon said.

"Okay. Good."

"We'll try it one more," Nixon said, "just to give you—" He
motioned with his hand to indicate he wanted the cameras
on. "Now, if you want, and then I'll give you a Buffalo."

Three beeps from the machine. Frank Shakespeare
stepped forward, not sure what was happening.

"Yeah, I'll try one more," Nixon told him.

"We're ready when you are, Mike," a floor man said.

"Okay, quiet on the floor, please. Here we go. We're ready
when you are, sir."

Nixon had it together now; all the phrases arranged properly in his mind. This was the finished product. This one would have cadence along with the statistics.

"As we enter the last few days of this campaign of nineteen sixty-eight, there's one issue on which there is a complete difference of opinion between the two candidates for President. And that's on the issue of law and order in the United States. Mr. Humphrey defends the record of the last four years, he defends the attorney general and his policies. I completely disagree." The headshake was more pronounced this time. "I say that when crime's been going up nine times as fast as population, when forty-three percent of the American people indicated in a recent poll that they're afraid to walk on the streets of their cities at night, we need a complete housecleaning in Washington. I pledge a new attorney general. I pledge an all-out war against organized crime in this country. I pledge that the first civil right of every American, the right to be free from domestic violence, will again be recognized and protected in this great country of ours."

He was finished.

"Okay," he said. "That gives you another two to play with. Now we'll try Buffalo."

Three beeps.

"This is again one minute?" Richard Nixon asked.

"Okay, Mike?" a floor man asked.

"Right, one minute. Quiet on the floor. Here we go, please. Ready when you are, sir."

Richard Nixon looked at the camera with an expression of concern on his face. *"Are the figures higher there?"* he had asked. "In reading some recent FBI statistics, I found that Buffalo and Erie County was one of the areas in the nation in which we've had an appalling rise in crime. I think we can do something about it. But we can't do something about it if we continue the old leadership. Mr. Humphrey pledges a continuation of that leadership. He defends the attorney general and his policies. I pledge a new attorney general. We will wage an all-out war against organized crime all over this nation. We're going to make the cities of our country, the streets of our country, free from fear again. With your help on November fifth, the first civil right of every American, the right to be free from domestic violence, will again be a right that you will have."

That "first civil right" line had not come back to him until the final version of the first commercial. But it pleased him so, the way it marched out of his mouth, that he was reluctant to abandon it. It was as if an old friend had paid him a surprise visit this gloomy morning.

"Let's try it once more," Richard Nixon said.

"Damned good," Frank Shakespeare said.

There were three beeps from the tape machine.

"Well, we can even use that, but we'll try it again," Nixon said.

Shakespeare stepped forward. "If you do this, and you end it again, say, 'it will again be a right that you will have here in Buffalo,' so that you'll have Buffalo—"

Richard Nixon was nodding. "Uh-huh. That's right."

"Ready when you are, Mike," the floor man said.

"Okay? Quiet, please, here we go again." Mike Stanislavsky looked at Nixon. "Ready when you are."

"In reading some recent FBI statistics, I found that Erie County and Buffalo was one of the areas in which there's been an appalling rise of crime over the past few years. I say that we have to stop this. In order to stop it we need new leadership from the top in the United States. Hubert Humphrey pledges to continue the old leadership. He defends the attorney general. And he defends the record of that attorney

general. I completely disagree. I say that we need a new attorney general, that we need to wage an all-out war against
organized crime in the United States of America. And I
pledge that under our new leadership we will again have
freedom from fear in America. We will again have for all
of the American people the protection of that first civil
right, and that is the right to be secure from domestic violence."

The cameras stopped.

"I think that's good," Nixon said. "What was the time on
that?"

"Forty-eight."

But there had been a technical problem. The siren of a
police car, trying to get through traffic on the street outside,
had been picked up on the tape.

"Cinéma vérité," someone said.

But Harry Treleaven considered it simply a flaw. From
the control room, word was sent up that the commercial
would have to be done again.

"Ask him why," Richard Nixon said.

"Tell him we had a technical problem," Garment said.

But that was not enough of an explanation.

"We don't want to do it again unless it's absolutely necessary," Frank Shakespeare said. He could see that Nixon's
mood, which had been considered exceptionally sunny until
now, was fading.

"It's absolutely necessary," Garment said from the control
room.

"Why?" Shakespeare said.

"You'd better go up and explain it, Len," Harry Treleaven
said.

Len Garment went upstairs. As he was on his way, Nixon
said to Shakespeare, "Make sure you ask him why, so then I'll

know what changes to make—if he wants a different tone or something."

"I don't know that we have to bother—" Shakespeare said.

"No, we'll do it," Nixon said.

Len Garment explained about the siren, assured Richard Nixon that his tone had been superb, and went back downstairs as Nixon again took his position on the edge of the desk. The tape machine beeped three times.

"Okay, Mike, we're ready."

"Okay, quiet on the floor, here we go again, please. Any time you're ready, sir."

"The latest FBI figures indicate that Erie County and Buffalo are one of the areas in which the greatest rise in crime has occurred— No, let's start again. Just keep right on."

Three beeps.

"Okay," the floor man said.

"All right," Richard Nixon said.

"Any time you're ready," Mike Stanislavsky said.

Nixon began, "In reading the—" He closed his eyes and winced.

"No," he said.

Three beeps from the machine.

"All right," Nixon said. "In reading the latest FBI figures I found that the most appalling rise in crime— Uh-uh. No."

He shook his head again. There were three more beeps from the tape machine. He looked at the floor again, steadying himself.

"Once more, then this'll do it," he said.

"Okay. Quiet, please. Here we go. Whenever you're ready."

"In reading the most recent FBI figures, one of the most appalling rises in crime in the whole country occurred in

Erie County and in Buffalo." Nixon was impatient now and plunged on despite that syntax. "I think we can do something about it. Hubert Humphrey pledges to continue the leadership of the past four years. He defends the attorney general and the record of the Department of Justice. I completely disagree. I say that we need a new attorney general. We need to wage an all-out war against organized crime in this country; we need to make secure that first civil right of all Americans, and that's the right to be secure from domestic violence. And to all of my friends in Buffalo, I say to you, you can help secure that right for you, for your neighbors, by your votes on November five. Vote for new leadership. Vote to throw out of office those who have failed to defend that right, the right to be secure from domestic violence."

He finished, delighted to be rid of the FBI statistics and the people of Buffalo and Erie County and their most appalling rise in crime.

"All right," he said. "That isn't important enough to do that often, but that's all right. But it's done now. That last one was a—" But his thought shifted suddenly.

"Now we'll do the southern one," he said.

"Tell me when you're ready," Mike Stanislavsky said.

Three beeps from the machine.

"This is another one-minute," Nixon said. He was feeling the pockets of his suitcoat. Then he began to look around on the desk top where he was sitting.

"Did you take them, Dwight?" he said to his personal aide. "My little notes I had here?"

Dwight Chapin said he had not.

"They were right on the table here."

There was a sixty-second pause while the notes were looked for and found. Then three beeps.

"We ready?"

"All right," Richard Nixon said. "We'll have to do this one probably twice, but—the timing, because I— Take a crack at it. Okay?"

"Stand by, please. Quiet on the floor. Ready any time you are, sir."

"There's been a lot of double-talk in the South about what is really at stake in this election in nineteen sixty-eight, and I think it's time for some straight talk. If there were a straight-up-and-down vote as to whether the people in the South wanted to continue for four more years the men who have led us for the last four years, whether they want Hubert Humphrey in the White House, the vote would be three to one against him. Only if that vote divides is it possible for Hubert Humphrey to be elected President of the United States. And that's why I say don't divide your vote on November five. Get the new leadership that America can have with our new team, leadership that will restore law and order, leadership that will bring peace abroad and keep peace abroad, leadership that will bring to America again progress without inflation and prosperity without war. Make your vote count."

Richard Nixon turned to Stanislavsky.

"What was that, fifty-two?"

"Exactly."

In the control room, Al Scott sighed with admiration. "Isn't that something?" he said. "He knew exactly how long he had gone. Without a watch. What a sense of timing."

"Yeah, well, you can try that one as one," Richard Nixon was saying. "And incidentally, use— Mix them up a little."

Shakespeare stepped forward. "Sure," he said. "Do you want to try this again?"

"Yeah, I'll do it again."

There were three beeps.

"This is a very important one to get out," Richard Nixon said.

"Yes, sir."

"And incidentally, you— Well, all right."

"Quiet on the floor, please," Stanislavsky said. "Here we go. Any time you're ready."

"There's been a lot of double-talk about the role of the South in the campaign of nineteen sixty-eight, and I think it's time for some straight talk. If there were a straight-up-and-down vote as to whether the people of the South wanted to continue in office those that have helped to make the policies of the last four years, in other words, whether they're for Hubert Humphrey for President, the vote would be three to one against him. Only if that vote divides is it possible for Hubert Humphrey to even have a chance to be elected the next President of the United States. And so I say, don't play their game. Don't divide your vote. Vote for the team, the only team that can provide the new leadership that America needs, the Nixon-Agnew team. And I pledge to you we will restore law and order in this country, we will bring peace abroad, and we will restore respect for America all over the world. And we will provide that prosperity without war, and progress without inflation that every American wants."

"That was even better," Frank Shakespeare said. "Those were good."

"Yeah, run them both," Nixon said. "Use them both."

He stood up.

"Now I'm going to go over to the side and get out of the light for a minute before the next."

He walked to the side of the stage.

"I sweat too much anyway," he said.

When he returned it was with the announcement that he wanted to do a special one-minute commercial about the New York City teachers' strike.

This had not been scheduled. It was Nixon's own idea, and to Harry Treleaven and Len Garment in the control room it seemed alarmingly inappropriate. Nixon had returned to the city from the campaign tour only the night before. To speak out suddenly about a local issue—and such a bitter issue as this—just two weeks before Election Day seemed unlikely to improve either the situation or Nixon's own image as a restrained and dispassionate chief executive-in-exile.

He again took his place at the edge of the desk.

"I—I'm going to do another one-minute, which—for New York City now, and—"

"Do that now?" Frank Shakespeare said.

"I'll do it now."

Shakespeare said something else.

"For New York City," Nixon said.

Mike Stanislavsky announced, "There's going to be one more one-minute for New York City."

"Okay, say when, Mike," the floor man said.

"Okay, stand by. Quiet on the floor, please, we're recording." He nodded toward Nixon. "When you're ready."

Nixon nodded back. "Uh-huh." The camera light came on.

"As I've traveled across the country I've found an immense interest and concern about the teachers' strike in New York City. Naturally, I'm not going to take a side—" No, that was the wrong way to put it.

"No, strike that," Nixon said. "I'll start again."

This time there were only two beeps.

"Okay, any time you're ready, sir."

"As I've campaigned across America these past few days,

I've found immense concern about the teachers' strike in New York City. Now, without getting into the merits of that controversy, I think that one point that should be emphasized that has not been emphasized enough is that the heart of the problem is law and order in our schools. I do not think that we can expect teachers to go into classrooms where there is not discipline and where they are not backed up by local school boards. It seems to me that when we ask somebody to teach our children we should give our teachers the backing that they deserve. Discipline in the classroom is essential if our children are to learn. It's essential if our teachers are to take up the obligation of teaching. Let's see to it that we do have law and order in the classrooms of America in the very best sense of the word. This is the only way for a better education for America's children."

There were two beeps from the tape machine. Downstairs, in the control room, Len Garment and Harry Treleaven looked at each other. Neither smiled. Garment shook his head back and forth with a quick, nervous motion.

"That's all right, Len," Treleaven said. "It'll never get on the air."

Upstairs, Frank Shakespeare had stepped forward to talk to Richard Nixon.

Nixon looked up at him.

"Yep," Richard Nixon said, "this hits it right on the nose, the thing about this whole teacher— It's all about law and order and the damn Negro–Puerto Rican groups out there."

Shakespeare looked at Richard Nixon.

"I don't care whether they're white or whoever the hell they are," Nixon said. "When they hit the teachers over the head, goddammit, they have no right to run the school. It's as simple as that. Okay, now we'll do the five-minute."

It was after noon when Richard Nixon left the studio. His friend from the Laugh-In show, Paul Keyes, was with him. Dwight Chapin and all the other men in short hair and dark suits who always followed him around also were there.

As he passed through the front lobby, a man from the Merv Griffin Show, a man who had known Nixon from the time he had been a guest on the show, stepped forward to wish him luck.

Richard Nixon stopped, accepted the handshake, and smiled. A man was holding open the door of the theater. Another man was holding open the door of Richard Nixon's car. The police had cleared a path through the small crowd that had formed outside the door.

"Say hi to everyone on the show for me," Richard Nixon said.

The man said he would.

"Oh, say, is that funny woman still on?"

The man from the show said he did not know what funny woman Richard Nixon meant.

"You know. The one with the funny voice."

The man gave a little shake of his head. He did not know what to say. Richard Nixon was the only one smiling. Everyone else was starting to get embarrassed.

"You know," Nixon persisted. "That funny lady."

The man looked past Richard Nixon, to the men who were with him. For help.

Paul Keyes stepped forward. From the Laugh-In show. He was a big man with gray hair and rimless glasses. The kind of Republican who thought John Wayne was good for the party.

"Oh, you mean Tiny Tim," Paul Keyes said to Richard

Nixon. And while everyone was laughing—Nixon, too—Paul Keyes motioned to the man at the door and the door was opened wider and Richard Nixon walked through and outside to where the cars were waiting.

◂2▸

Politics, in a sense, has always been a con game.

The American voter, insisting upon his belief in a higher order, clings to his religion, which promises another, better life; and defends passionately the illusion that the men he chooses to lead him are of finer nature than he.

It has been traditional that the successful politician honor this illusion. To succeed today, he must embellish it. Particularly if he wants to be President.

"Potential presidents are measured against an ideal that's a combination of leading man, God, father, hero, pope, king, with maybe just a touch of the avenging Furies thrown in," an adviser to Richard Nixon wrote in a memorandum late in 1967. Then, perhaps aware that Nixon qualified only as father, he discussed improvements that would have to be made —not upon Nixon himself, but upon the image of him which was received by the voter.

That there is a difference between the individual and his image is human nature. Or American nature, at least. That the difference is exaggerated and exploited electronically is the reason for this book.

Advertising, in many ways, is a con game, too. Human beings do not need new automobiles every third year; a color television set brings little enrichment of the human experience; a higher or lower hemline no expansion of consciousness, no increase in the capacity to love.

It is not surprising then, that politicians and advertising men should have discovered one another. And, once they recognized that the citizen did not so much vote for a candidate as make a psychological purchase of him, not surprising that they began to work together.

The voter, as reluctant to face political reality as any other kind, was hardly an unwilling victim. "The deeper problems connected with advertising," Daniel Boorstin has written in *The Image,* "come less from the unscrupulousness of our 'deceivers' than from our pleasure in being deceived, less from the desire to seduce than from the desire to be seduced. . . .

"In the last half-century we have misled ourselves . . . about men . . . and how much greatness can be found among them. . . . We have become so accustomed to our illusions that we mistake them for reality. We demand them. And we demand that there be always more of them, bigger and better and more vivid."

The Presidency seems the ultimate extension of our error.

Advertising agencies have tried openly to sell Presidents since 1952. When Dwight Eisenhower ran for re-election in 1956, the agency of Batton, Barton, Durstine and Osborn, which had been on a retainer throughout his first four years, accepted his campaign as a regular account. Leonard Hall, national Republican chairman, said: "You sell your candidates and your programs the way a business sells its products."

The only change over the past twelve years has been that,

as technical sophistication has increased, so has circumspection. The ad men were removed from the parlor but were given a suite upstairs.

What Boorstin says of advertising: "It has meant a reshaping of our very concept of truth," is particularly true of advertising on TV.

With the coming of television, and the knowledge of how it could be used to seduce voters, the old political values disappeared. Something new, murky, undefined started to rise from the mists. "In all countries," Marshall McLuhan writes, "the party system has folded like the organization chart. Policies and issues are useless for election purposes, since they are too specialized and hot. The shaping of a candidate's integral image has taken the place of discussing conflicting points of view."

Americans have never quite digested television. The mystique which should fade grows stronger. We make celebrities not only of the men who cause events but of the men who read reports of them aloud.

The televised image can become as real to the housewife as her husband, and much more attractive. Hugh Downs is a better breakfast companion, Merv Griffin cozier to snuggle with on the couch.

Television, in fact, has given status to the "celebrity" which few real men attain. And the "celebrity" here is the one described by Boorstin: "Neither good nor bad, great nor petty . . . the human pseudo-event . . . fabricated on purpose to satisfy our exaggerated expectations of human, greatness."

This is, perhaps, where the twentieth century and its pursuit of illusion have been leading us. "In the last half-century," Boorstin writes, "the old heroic human mold has been broken. A new mold has been made, so that marketable human models—modern 'heroes'—could be mass-produced, to satisfy the market, and without any hitches. The qualities which now commonly make a man or woman into a 'nationally advertised' brand are in fact a new category of human emptiness."

The television celebrity is a vessel. An inoffensive container in which someone else's knowledge, insight, compassion, or wit can be presented. And we respond like the child on Christmas morning who ignores the gift to play with the wrapping paper.

Television seems particularly useful to the politician who can be charming but lacks ideas. Print is for ideas. Newspapermen write not about people but policies; the paragraphs can be slid around like blocks. Everyone is colored gray. Columnists—and commentators in the more polysyllabic magazines—concentrate on ideology. They do not care what a man sounds like; only how he thinks. For the candidate who does not, such exposure can be embarrassing. He needs another way to reach the people.

On television it matters less that he does not have ideas. His personality is what the viewers want to share. He need be neither statesman nor crusader; he must only show up on time. Success and failure are easily measured: how often is he invited back? Often enough and he reaches his goal—to advance from "politician" to "celebrity," a status jump bestowed by grateful viewers who feel that finally they have been given the basis for making a choice.

The TV candidate, then, is measured not against his predecessors—not against a standard of performance established by two centuries of democracy—but against Mike Douglas. How well does he handle himself? Does he mumble, does he twitch, does he make me laugh? Do I feel warm inside?

Style becomes substance. The medium is the massage and the masseur gets the votes.

In office, too, the ability to project electronically is essential. We were willing to forgive John Kennedy his Bay of Pigs; we followed without question the perilous course on which he led us when missiles were found in Cuba; we even tolerated his calling of reserves for the sake of a bluff about Berlin.

We forgave, followed, and accepted because we liked the way he looked. And he had a pretty wife. Camelot was fun, even for the peasants, as long as it was televised to their huts.

Then came Lyndon Johnson, heavy and gross, and he was forgiven nothing. He might have survived the sniping of the displaced intellectuals had he only been able to charm. But no one taught him how. Johnson was syrupy. He stuck to the lens. There was no place for him in our culture.

"The success of any TV performer depends on his achieving a low-pressure style of presentation," McLuhan has written. The harder a man tries, the better he must hide it. Television demands gentle wit, irony, understatement: the qualities of Eugene McCarthy. The TV politician cannot make a speech; he must engage in intimate conversation. He must never press. He should suggest, not state; request, not demand. Nonchalance is the key word. Carefully studied nonchalance.

Warmth and sincerity are desirable but must be handled with care. Unfiltered, they can be fatal. Television did great harm to Hubert Humphrey. His excesses—talking too long and too fervently, which were merely annoying in an auditorium—became lethal in a television studio. The performer must talk to one person at a time. He is brought into the living room. He is a guest. It is improper for him to shout. Humphrey vomited on the rug.

It would be extremely unwise for the TV politician to admit such knowledge of his medium. The necessary nonchalance should carry beyond his appearance while *on* the show; it should rule his attitude *toward* it. He should express distaste for television; suspicion that there is something "phony" about it. This guarantees him good press, because newspaper reporters, bitter over their loss of prestige to the television men, are certain to stress anti-television remarks. Thus, the sophisticated candidate, while analyzing his own on-the-air technique as carefully as a golf pro studies his swing, will state frequently that there is no place for "public relations gimmicks" or "those show business guys" in his campaign. Most of the television men working for him will be unbothered by such remarks. They are willing to accept anonymity, even scorn, as long as the pay is good.

Into this milieu came Richard Nixon: grumpy, cold, and aloof. He would claim privately that he lost elections because the American voter was an adolescent whom he tried to treat as an adult. Perhaps. But if he treated the voter as an adult, it was as an adult he did not want for a neighbor.

This might have been excused had he been a man of genuine vision. An explorer of the spirit. Martin Luther King, for instance, got by without being one of the boys. But Richard Nixon did not strike people that way. He had, in Richard Rovere's words, "an advertising man's approach to his work," acting as if he believed "policies [were] products to be sold the public—this one today, that one tomorrow, depending on the discounts and the state of the market."

So his enemies had him on two counts: his personality, and the convictions—or lack of such—which lay behind. They worked him over heavily on both.

Norman Mailer remembered him as "a church usher, of the variety who would twist a boy's ear after removing him from church."

McLuhan watched him debate Kennedy and thought he resembled "the railway lawyer who signs leases that are not in the best interests of the folks in the little town."

But Nixon survived, despite his flaws, because he was tough and smart, and—some said—dirty when he had to be. Also, because there was nothing else he knew. A man to whom politics is all there is in life will almost always beat one to whom it is only an occupation.

He nearly became President in 1960, and that year it would not have been by default. He failed because he was too few of the things a President had to be—and, because he had no press to lie for him and did not know how to use television to lie about himself.

It was just Nixon and John Kennedy and they sat down together in a television studio and a little red light began to glow and Richard Nixon was finished. Television would be blamed but for all the wrong reasons.

They would say it was makeup and lighting, but Nixon's problem went deeper than that. His problem was himself. Not what he said but the man he was. The camera portrayed him clearly. America took its Richard Nixon straight and did not like the taste.

The content of the programs made little difference. Except for startling lapses, content seldom does. What mattered was the image the viewers received, though few observers at the time caught the point.

McLuhan read Theodore White's *The Making of The President* book and was appalled at the section on the debates. "White offers statistics on the number of sets in American homes and the number of hours of daily use of these sets, but not one clue as to the nature of the TV image or its effects on candidates or viewers. White considers the 'content' of the debates and the deportment of the debaters, but it never occurs to him to ask why TV would inevitably be a disaster for a sharp intense image like Nixon's and a boon for the blurry, shaggy texture of Kennedy." In McLuhan's opinion: "Without TV, Nixon had it made."

What the camera showed was Richard Nixon's hunger. He lost, and bitter, confused, he blamed it on his beard.

He made another, lesser thrust in 1962, and that failed, too. He showed the world a little piece of his heart the morning after and then he moved East to brood. They did not want him, the hell with them. He was going to Wall Street and get rich.

He was afraid of television. He knew his soul was hard to find. Beyond that, he considered it a gimmick; its use in politics offended him. It had not been part of the game when he had learned to play, he could see no reason to bring it in now. He half suspected it was an eastern liberal trick: one more way to make him look silly. It offended his sense of dignity, one of the truest senses he had.

So his decision to use it to become President in 1968 was not easy. So much of him argued against it. But in his Wall Street years, Richard Nixon had traveled to the darkest places inside himself and come back numbed. He was, as in the Graham Greene title, a burnt-out case. All feeling was behind him; the machine inside had proved his hardiest part. He would run for President again and if he would have to learn television to run well, then he would learn it.

America still saw him as the 1960 Nixon. If he were to come at the people again, as candidate, it would have to be as something new; not this scarred, discarded figure from their past.

He spoke to men who thought him mellowed. They detected growth, a new stability, a sense of direction that had been lacking. He would return with fresh perspective, a more unselfish urgency.

His problem was how to let the nation know. He could not do it through the press. He knew what to expect from them, which was the same as he had always gotten. He would have to circumvent them. Distract them with coffee and dough-nuts and smiles from his staff and tell his story another way.

Television was the only answer, despite its sins against him in the past. But not just any kind of television. An un-committed camera could do irreparable harm. His television would have to be controlled. He would need experts. They would have to find the proper settings for him, or if they could not be found, manufacture them. These would have to be men of keen judgment and flawless taste. He was, after all, Richard Nixon, and there were certain things he could not do. Wearing love beads was one. He would need men of dig-nity. Who believed in him and shared his vision. But more importantly, men who knew television as a weapon: from broadest concept to most technical detail. This would be Richard Nixon, the leader, returning from exile. Perhaps not beloved, but respected. Firm but not harsh; just but compas-sionate. With flashes of warmth spaced evenly throughout.

Nixon gathered about himself a group of young men attuned to the political uses of television. They arrived at his
side by different routes. One, William Gavin, was a thirty-
one-year-old English teacher in a suburban high school outside Philadelphia in 1967, when he wrote Richard Nixon a
letter urging him to run for President and base his campaign
on TV. Gavin wrote on stationery borrowed from the University of Pennsylvania because he thought Nixon would pay
more attention if the letter seemed to be from a college professor.

Dear Mr. Nixon:

May I offer two suggestions concerning your plans for 1968?

1. Run. You can win. Nothing can happen to you, politically
speaking, that is worse than what has happened to you. Ortega y
Gassett in his *The Revolt of the Masses* says: "These ideas are the
only genuine ideas; the ideas of the shipwrecked. All the rest is
rhetoric, posturing, farce. He who does not really feel himself lost,
is lost without remission . . ." You, in effect, are "lost"; that is
why you are the only political figure with the vision to see things
the way they are and not as Leftist or Rightist kooks would have
them be. Run. You will win.

2. A tip for television: instead of those wooden performances beloved by politicians, instead of a glamorboy technique, instead of
safety, be bold. Why not have live press conferences as your campaign on television? People will see you daring all, asking and
answering questions from reporters, and not simply answering
phony "questions" made up by your staff. This would be dynamic;
it would be daring. Instead of the medium using you, you would
be using the medium. Go on "live" and risk all. It is the only way
to convince people of the truth: that you are beyond rhetoric, that
you can face reality, unlike your opponents, who will rely on public relations. Television hurt you because you were not yourself; it
didn't hurt the "real" Nixon. The real Nixon can revolutionize the

35

use of television by dynamically going "live" and answering everything, the loaded and the unloaded question. Invite your opponents to this kind of a debate.

Good luck, and I know you can win if you see yourself for what you are; a man who had been beaten, humiliated, hated, but who can still see the truth.

A Nixon staff member had lunch with Gavin a couple of times after the letter was received and hired him. Gavin began churning out long, stream-of-consciousness memos which dealt mostly with the importance of image, and ways in which Richard Nixon, through television, could acquire a good one.

"Voters are basically lazy, basically uninterested in making an *effort* to understand what we're talking about . . . ," Gavin wrote. "Reason requires a high degree of discipline, of concentration; impression is easier. Reason pushes the viewer back, it assaults him, it demands that he agree or disagree; impression can envelop him, invite him in, without making an intellectual demand. . . . When we argue with him we demand that he make the effort of replying. We seek to engage his intellect, and for most people this is the most difficult work of all. The emotions are more easily roused, closer to the surface, more malleable. . . ."

So, for the New Hampshire primary, Gavin recommended "saturation with a film, in which the candidate can be shown better than he can be shown in person because it can be edited, so only the best moments are shown; then a quick parading of the candidate in the flesh so that the guy they've gotten intimately acquainted with on the screen takes on a living presence—not saying anything, just being seen. . . .

"[Nixon] has to come across as a person larger than life, the stuff of legend. People are stirred by the legend, including the living legend, not by the man himself. It's the aura that surrounds the charismatic figure more than it is the figure itself, that draws the followers. Our task is to build that aura. . . .

"So let's not be afraid of television gimmicks . . . get the voters to like the guy and the battle's two-thirds won."

William Gavin was brought to the White House as a speech writer in January of 1969.

Harry Treleaven, hired as creative director of advertising in the fall of 1967, immediately went to work on the more serious of Nixon's personality problems. One was his lack of humor.

"Can be corrected to a degree," Treleaven wrote, "but let's not be too obvious about it. Romney's cornball attempts have hurt him. If we're going to be witty, let a pro write the words."

Treleaven also worried about Nixon's lack of warmth, but decided that "he can be helped greatly in this respect by how he is handled. . . . Give him words to say that will show his *emotional* involvement in the issues. . . . Buchanan wrote about RFK talking about the starving children in Recife. *That's* what we have to inject. . . .

"He should be presented in some kind of 'situation' rather than cold in a studio. The situation should look unstaged even if it's not."

Some of the most effective ideas belonged to Raymond K. Price, a former editorial writer for the *New York Herald Tribune,* who became Nixon's best and most prominent speech writer in the campaign. Price later composed much of the inaugural address.

In 1967, he began with the assumption that, "The natural human use of reason is to support prejudice, not to arrive at opinions." Which led to the conclusion that rational arguments would "only be effective if we can get the people to make the *emotional* leap, or what theologians call [the] 'leap of faith.' "

Price suggested attacking the "personal factors" rather than the "historical factors" which were the basis of the low opinion so many people had of Richard Nixon.

"These tend to be more a gut reaction," Price wrote, "unarticulated, non-analytical, a product of the particular chemistry between the voter and the *image* of the candidate. *We have to be very clear on this point: that the response is to the image, not to the man.* . . . It's not what's *there* that counts, it's what's projected—and carrying it one step further, it's not what *he* projects but rather what the voter receives. It's not the man we have to change, but rather the *received impression*. And this impression often depends more on the medium and its use than it does on the candidate himself."

So there would not have to be a "new Nixon." Simply a new approach to television.

"What, then, does this mean in terms of our uses of time and of media?" Price wrote.

"For one thing, it means investing whatever time RN needs in order to work out firmly in his own mind that vision of the nation's future that he wants to be identified with. This is crucial. . . ."

So, at the age of fifty-four, after twenty years in public life, Richard Nixon was still felt *by his own staff* to be in need of time to "work out firmly in his own mind that vision of the nation's future that he wants to be identified with."

"Secondly," Price wrote, "it suggests that we take the time and the money to experiment, in a controlled manner, with film and television techniques, with particular emphasis on pinpointing those *controlled* uses of the television medium that can *best* convey the *image* we want to get across . . .

38

"The TV medium itself introduces an element of distortion, in terms of its effect on the candidate and of the often subliminal ways in which the image is received. And it inevitably is going to convey a partial image—thus ours is the task of finding how to control its use so the part that gets across is the part we want to have gotten across. . . ."

So this was how they went into it. Trying, with one hand, to build the illusion that Richard Nixon, in addition to his attributes of mind and heart, considered, in the words of Patrick K. Buchanan, a speech writer, "communicating with the people . . . one of the great joys of seeking the Presidency"; while with the other they shielded him, controlled him, and controlled the atmosphere around him. It was as if they were building not a President but an Astrodome, where the wind would never blow, the temperature never rise or fall, and the ball never bounce erratically on the artificial grass.

They could do this, and succeed, because of the special nature of the man. There was, apparently, something in Richard Nixon's character which sought this shelter. Something which craved regulation, which flourished best in the darkness, behind clichés, behind phalanxes of antiseptic advisers. Some part of him that could breathe freely only inside a hotel suite that cost a hundred dollars a day.

And it worked. As he moved serenely through his primary campaign, there was new cadence to Richard Nixon's speech and motion; new confidence in his heart. And, a new image of him on the television screen.

TV both reflected and contributed to his strength. Because he was winning he looked like a winner on the screen. Because he was suddenly projecting well on the medium he had feared, he went about his other tasks with assurance. The one fed upon the other, building to an astonishing peak in August as the Republican convention began and he emerged from his regal isolation, traveling to Miami not so much to be nominated as coronated. On live, but controlled, TV.

◄3►

I FIRST MET Harry Treleaven on a rainy morning in June of 1968, in his office at Fuller and Smith and Ross, the advertising agency, on the thirty-seventh floor of 666 Fifth Avenue in New York.

Treleaven was small and thin. He had gray hair and the tight, frowning mouth that you see on the assistant principal of a high school. He seemed to be in his middle forties. He looked like William Scranton.

A story in the *Times* that morning about Richard Nixon's new image had mentioned his name.

"But they spelled it wrong," he said.

He was annoyed. I thought then it was his pride. Later I would discover it was at the idea that such inefficiency could exist in so high a place. If they dropped the second "e" from Treleaven, how could they be trusted to judge the Chinese?

Treleaven, it turned out, did not work for Fuller and Smith and Ross. He worked for Richard Nixon. Fuller and Smith and Ross was only incidental to the campaign. An agency was needed to do the mechanics—buying the television time and the newspaper space.

Treleaven had been born in Chicago and had gone to Duke University, where he graduated Phi Beta Kappa. After that, he moved to Los Angeles and worked on the *Los Angeles Times* and then wrote radio scripts.

One night he and his wife were having dinner in a restaurant in Los Angeles with a couple he did not like. Halfway through the meal, he turned to his wife.

"Do you like it here?"

"You mean the restaurant?"

"I mean Los Angeles."

"No, not especially."

"Then let's go."

And Harry Treleaven threw a twenty-dollar bill on the table and he and his wife walked out. He took a plane to New York that night.

He found a job with the J. Walter Thompson advertising agency. "Only temporary," he said: taken only because his wife was pregnant and he needed steady pay.

He stayed with Thompson eighteen years. When he left it was as a vice president. He did commercials for Pan American, RCA, Ford, and Lark cigarettes, among others.

Harry Treleaven would travel often to Los Angeles for the agency. On certain trips he would call a man he once had worked for on the *Los Angeles Times*. "I'm paying more in alimony now than you paid me in salary," he would say, "if that can be considered a sign of success."

A few notes from a biographical sketch of Harry Treleaven prepared for the J. Walter Thompson company newspaper portray him as well as can be done.

No one has ever seen him work with his coat off . . . his clothes say Brooks Brothers but he buys them somewhere else. . . . He doesn't talk much. He has a thing for the hills of Vermont, for instance, especially in the fall, but ask him how it went last time around and he'll give you a cryptic "short" . . . (In advertising) the plan, the argument, the attitude, the atmosphere are more his *metier* (than the actual writing). . . . He loves old things like whaling ships—his first house in Amagansett was built by a whaling skipper 175 years ago—yet he's preoccupied with *au courant.* . . . He likes to spot a fresh trend and get you to go along. He is caught up with the crowd and what makes it go but rarely goes with it. . . . He owns the image of a swinger but he rarely stays up late enough to catch the 11 o'clock news. . . . He admires people who seem to come by their style without really trying. The British for instance—"They always make me feel inferior"—He is something of a stoic. Raised as a Christian Scientist, he never took medicine until he was 21. . . . He's taught himself to let an ad die without letting it kill him, and takes vacations lightly. It's not unusual for him to take three days off and come in to the office for one. . . .

The only thing I can think to add is that he loves artificial plants. During September and October, when Gene Jones, the man who was making the sixty-second spots, was working out of a studio at First Avenue and Fifty-third Street, Harry Treleaven would walk to see him almost every day. There was an artificial flower and plant store on the way. He would stop, whenever he had time, and browse tenderly, as one might in a bookstore. What impressed him most, he said, was how skillfully something artificial could be made.

He took a leave of absence from J. Walter Thompson in 1966, to work on a congressional campaign in Texas. The candidate was George Bush, forty-two years old, native of Massachusetts, graduate of Yale, and son of former Senator Prescott Bush of Connecticut. Bush was running in a district in Houston from which no Republican ever had been elected. Two years earlier he had run against Ralph Yarborough for the Senate and lost.

His campaign manager, Jimmy Allison, had known Harry Treleaven a long time. Now he called New York to ask if Treleaven would direct the advertising of the campaign. Tre-

leaven was bored in New York. A political campaign looked
like fun. Besides, George Bush had plenty of money and was
ready to spend it. Treleaven said yes.

A poll, taken in July, showed the incumbent, Frank Briscoe, leading, 49 percent to 41. But Treleaven saw three
promising signs: Briscoe was overconfident, dull, and un-
loved; Bush was a good campaigner (in the Senate race he
had received 43.6 percent of the vote, the best Republican
showing for major office in Texas history); and, most important, Bush knew that the red light meant the television camera was on.

Later, in the winter following the campaign, Treleaven
wrote a long report of what he had done. He called it "Upset:
The Story of a Modern Political Campaign," and had seven
copies made. He had written of himself in the third person:
"Treleaven, of course, looked long and carefully at candidate
George Bush. What he saw he liked—and, more importantly,
he recognized that what he liked was highly promotable."

One thing that intrigued Treleaven was that issues would
not have to be involved in the campaign. There was no issue
when it came to selling Ford automobiles; there were only
the product, the competition and the advertising. He saw no
reason why politics should be any different.

He wrote in "Upset," "Most national issues today are so
complicated, so difficult to understand, and have opinions on
that they either intimidate or, more often, bore the average
voter. . . . Few politicians recognize this fact."

Harry Treleaven went around Houston in the August heat,
asking people on the street what they thought of George
Bush. He found that Bush was "an extremely likeable person," but that "there was a haziness about exactly where he
stood politically."

This was perfect. "There'll be few opportunities for logical

44

persuasion," Treleaven wrote, "which is all right—because probably more people vote for irrational, emotional reasons than professional politicians suspect."

So there were no issues in the race. Not even when poor Briscoe, when asked publicly if he would favor negotiations with the NLF to end the Vietnamese war, said he did not know what the NLF was.

"Political candidates are celebrities," Treleaven wrote, "and today, with television taking them into everybody's home right along with Johnny Carson and Batman, they're more of a public attraction than ever."

Eighty percent of George Bush's campaign budget went to advertising. Fifty-nine percent of this went to television. Newspapers got 3 percent.

The fact that Bush was behind, Treleaven felt, was good. "We can turn this into an advantage," he wrote, "by creating a 'fighting underdog' image. Bush must convince voters that he really wants to be elected and is working hard to earn their vote. *People sympathize with a man who tries hard:* they are also flattered that anyone would really exert himself to get their vote. Bush, therefore, must be shown as a man who's working his heart out to win."

And he was. Over and over again, on every television screen in Houston, George Bush was seen with his coat slung over a shoulder; his sleeves rolled up; walking the streets of his district; grinning, gripping, sweating, letting the voter know he cared. About what, was never made clear.

George Bush defeated Frank Briscoe with 58 percent of the vote to 42. Harry Treleaven decided to stay in politics.

He was sitting on the beach at Amagansett one day in September of 1967, drinking a can of beer. Alone. A summer neighbor named Len Garment, who was a partner in the law firm where Richard Nixon worked, approached him. Len Garment's two kids were with him. His wife was packing to move back to the city for the winter and she wanted them all out of the house. Harry Treleaven knew Garment from a meeting they had had earlier in the summer. Garment had vaguely mentioned something about Treleaven and the advertising needs of the Richard Nixon campaign. Now he was more specific. He offered Treleaven a job. Creative director of advertising. Treleaven would devise a theme for the campaign, create commercials to fit the theme, and see that they were produced with a maximum of professional skill. Treleaven said he would think about it and call Garment in New York. Within a month they made a deal.

Len Garment's office was on the third floor of Nixon headquarters, at Park Avenue and Fifty-seventh Street. A man named Jim Howard, a public relations man from Cleveland, was with him the day I came in. Jim Howard was talking to Wilt Chamberlain on the phone.

"Wilt, I *understand* your position, but they just don't pay that kind of money. . . ."

Garment was a short, pudgy man, also in his middle forties, who once had played saxophone in a Woody Herman band. He had voted for John Kennedy in 1960. Then he met Nixon at the law firm. Garment was chief of litigation and he was making money, but he hated the job. He found that Nixon was not so bad a guy and very smart. When Nixon asked him to work in the presidential campaign, he said yes. He had been practically the first person to be hired and now he was chief recruiter.

"We went to Harry Treleaven," he said, "because of his

experience with the great institutional products of America. This was just the kind of man we wanted. Very sound. Non-gimmicky. Twenty years of experience with J. Walter Thompson, the biggest agency in the country. He handled Pan Am, Ford, RCA—as I said, the established American institutions."

Jim Howard finally hung up the phone.

"Well?"

"I don't know. He told me to call him back."

Jim Howard was trying to get Wilt Chamberlain to appear on the Mike Douglas Show for free. The idea was for Chamberlain to explain why Richard Nixon should be President. Chamberlain was the only Negro celebrity they had and they were trying to get him around. The problem was, the Douglas show did not pay. And Chamberlain wanted money.

Len Garment started to explain the Nixon approach to advertising. Or the Garment-Treleaven approach to advertising Nixon.

"The big thing is to stay away from gimmicks," he said.

"Right," Jim Howard said. "Never let the candidate wear a hat he does not feel comfortable wearing. You can't sell the candidate like a product," he said. "A product, all you want to do is get attention. You only need two percent additional buyers to make the campaign worthwhile. In politics you need a flat fifty-one percent of the market and you can't get that through gimmicks."

Two weeks later, I met Frank Shakespeare. Treleaven, Garment, who in June of 1969 was named special assistant to the President in the area of civil rights, and Shakespeare made up what was called the media and advertising group. But of the three equals, Shakespeare was quickly becoming more equal than the others.

He had come from CBS. He, too, was in his forties, with

blond hair and a soft, boyish face. When he was named director of the United States Information Agency, after Nixon's
election, a *New York Times* profile reported that, although
he had spent eighteen years at CBS, no one he had worked
with there could recall a single anecdote about him. "Not
exactly the kind of man you'd follow into the fire," a former
colleague said.

Shakespeare was working for free, because his progress at
CBS had been stalled when Jim Aubrey got fired. He had
been one of Aubrey's boys. Now, it was said, he was trying to
give his career some outside impetus. An association with the
President of the United States could hardly hurt.

◄4►

ON AUGUST 21, the morning after the Russians invaded Czechoslovakia, Harry Treleaven got to his office early. He was in an exceptionally good mood. It was the invasion. It had proved Nixon was right all along. The Russians had not changed.

"Makes it kind of hard to be a dove, doesn't it?" he said, smiling.

Treleaven was leaving for Teletape right away. The day before, he had cut Nixon's forty-five-minute acceptance speech to thirty minutes. Frank Shakespeare wanted to put it on the air that weekend, but he wanted to see it first.

Len Garment was at the studio when Treleaven got there. "What about this Czech thing?" he said. He looked really worried. Treleaven smiled. "Oh, I don't know, Len. Look at the positive side."

"Well, yes," Garment said. "I think it will bring a restoration of realism to American political discussion."

But Treleaven had been thinking of something else. "Unless we make some really colossal mistake," he said, "I don't see how we can lose."

Then Shakespeare came in. He was exuberant.

"What a break!" he said. "This Czech thing is just perfect. It puts the soft-liners in a hell of a box!"

Harry Treleaven had used the CBS tape of the acceptance

speech to make the commercial. "Better camera angles," he explained. "And besides, NBC has a peculiar form of editorializing. For instance, they'll cut to some young colored guy who's not applauding while Nixon talks of bridges to human dignity."

In the beginning of the acceptance speech, Richard Nixon had made a sweeping motion with his arm and shouted, "Let's win this one for Ike!" and all the Republicans cheered. Harry Treleaven had cut this line from the speech.

"Good," Shakespeare said. "Very good, Harry. That's the one line Rose Mary Woods wanted out of there." Rose Mary Woods was Richard Nixon's secretary. Because she had stuck with him through all the bad years, she emerged in 1968 as an adviser, too.

"She read the speech before he gave it and she said there was just one line he shouldn't utter, and that was it," Shakespeare said. "Usually, he listens to her but this time he insisted."

Another thing Harry Treleaven had cut was a reference to "the era of negotiation" with the Russians. Shakespeare was very happy this had gone. It would have been awful, he thought—they all thought—to have a reference to negotiations now that this invasion had occurred. This was the Cold War again, and adrenalin was flowing.

A big meeting was scheduled at Fuller and Smith and Ross for lunchtime. The agency had ordered ham sandwiches with a lot of lettuce and big pots of coffee. Everyone sat down and took little bites out of their sandwiches while Frank Shakespeare stood up and talked.

Already, there was bad feeling between the agency people and the Nixon group. In the beginning, the agency had believed it actually was going to create commercials. Then Harry Treleaven walked in. Without even saying good morning. Now the agency was making money but it was embarrassed. Treleaven would not tell them what he was doing. "No need to," he said.

That morning, in fact, just before Treleaven left for the film studio, the president of the agency, Art Duram, a tall, sad-faced, white-haired man who smoked a pipe, had appeared in the doorway of Treleaven's office.

"Well, Harry, what are we going to be doing now?" he said.

"Well, Art, we're just going to start producing commercials."

"What kind of commercials?"

"We haven't decided yet."

"Well, Harry, don't you think we'd better start putting things together?"

"Don't worry about it, Art. I've got ideas in my head."

"We've got to worry about it, Harry. You're talking about spending ten million dollars between now and the election and if we keep putting on the same commercials every day— that acceptance speech over and over again—they're going to start hurting us."

"The use of the speech ends September one."

"Then we have to create some new things."

"Yes, Art, I'm aware of that."

"I mean we can't keep using that speech. It will drive people out of their minds, hearing the same thing over and over again."

"I know, Art."

Harry Treleaven began to write on a pad. Art Duram stood in the doorway a few seconds longer and then, when Treleaven did not look up, he went away.

Now Art Duram sat at the table, waiting for the meeting to start. He was in an uncomfortable position, exposed, at meetings like this. All these people who worked for him at Fuller and Smith and Ross sitting there, watching the Nixon crowd talk to him.

Harry Treleaven said he had been thinking it over, and rather than rush something new into production he would prefer to continue the sixty-second excerpts from the acceptance speech that had been running as radio commercials.

Art Duram immediately lit his pipe. "But your exposure on that speech . . . ," he said. "You're going to be horrendously overexposed."

"I'm not sure that's bad, Art," Treleaven said. "He's saying some awfully good things."

"But psychologically—"

"Well, the problem is, we have nothing else to use and there's nothing else we could have ready that quickly unless it were a real emergency and I just don't think it is."

Duram shrugged.

Then a red-haired lady named Ruth Jones spoke up from the other side of the table. She had been hired by Shakespeare to supervise the buying of television and radio time for the commercials.

"Nixon should go on the air tonight with a special broadcast about Czechoslovakia," she said.

Shakespeare shook his head. "He'd have to be too good. He couldn't get ready. He's better off not saying anything. He's been Mr. Cool and Mr. Calm through this whole thing."

"But he could be Mr. Cool and Mr. Calm and still make a very effective speech."

"He can't, Ruth. There just isn't time. It might be a very good idea but I know right now what the reaction would be if it were brought up at headquarters. And there's no point in disturbing anyone unnecessarily."

Ruth Jones shrugged. "I still think he should do it," she

said. "But let's move on to something else—we're going to get bold listings in the *Times* starting immediately."

"Bold listings?" Shakespeare said.

"Yes, in the TV section. Listing our commercials in bold type in the schedule. They had been doing it for McCarthy and not for us. But I tossed a couple of hand grenades. At the networks *and* the *Times*. And I got immediate results."

Then a man walked into the room with a big colored poster under his arm. The poster was a close-up picture of Richard Nixon smiling. Beneath it were the words: THIS TIME VOTE LIKE YOUR WHOLE WORLD DEPENDED ON IT.

"This is the new slogan," he said. "And together with the picture, this will run in the center spread of *Life* Magazine and on our billboards."

Frank Shakespeare was staring at the picture.

"Do you like the photograph?" he said, turning toward Len Garment.

"I have a little bit of a problem with that tremendous smile, tied in with the serious line," Garment said.

The man with the poster was nodding. "We're still looking for the right picture," he said, "and it's difficult. But this expression is not a laugh to me. It's a youthful expression. It has vitality. To look at it inspires confidence. The picture has sensitivity, and one of the reasons we ran the line behind him —in back of his head—is so he wouldn't appear to be speaking it. See, it's there, but just as part of the image. The connection is not direct."

"Yes," Frank Shakespeare said. "All right."

"It will make a tremendous billboard," Treleaven said.

"There's character in the face," Shakespeare said.

"We've got the best-looking candidate, no doubt about it," Treleaven said.

"So it's a cheerful, grim, serious, and optimistic picture," Len Garment said, smiling.

"And youthful," Shakespeare added.

"Ah," said Ruth Jones, who still wanted him to speak on Czechoslovakia, "a man for all seasons."

Then they talked about fund raising.

"The first McCarthy telecast raised a hundred and twenty-five thousand dollars," Ruth Jones said.

"Who gave the pitch?" Shakespeare asked.

"Paul Newman."

"Oh, well, that made a difference."

"It was a personal involvement pitch. Dick Goodwin wrote it for him."

"We'll use the same pitch," Shakespeare said, "but we don't have as strong a man."

"Who do we have?"

"Bud Wilkinson."

At four o'clock, Treleaven walked to a west side theater to look at a film that had been made with Spiro Agnew at Mission Bay, California, the week after the convention.

"It could be a great help, particularly with Agnew, if it's any good," Treleaven said.

"What have you done about Agnew so far?"

"Done?" Treleaven said. "Nothing. He's just there."

"Are you happy about him?"

"He doesn't bother me as much as he does some people."

Shakespeare and Garment already were at the theater. So was the man who had made the films: a TV documentary man whom Shakespeare had hired especially for this job. He was wearing sneakers and shifting nervously from foot to

THE SELLING OF THE PRESIDENT 1968

foot. There were two separate films, each containing an interview with one of the candidates. The Agnew film was shown first.

It had been shot in color, with sailboats in the blue bay as a backdrop. Agnew was squinting in the sun.

"All life," he said, "is essentially the contributions that come from compromise." His voice was sleepy, his face without expression. The questions fit right in.

"It must have really been a thrill to have been picked for Vice President. Were you happy?"

"The ability to be happy is directly proportional to the ability to suffer," Agnew said. His tone indicated he might doze before finishing the sentence, "and as you grow older you feel everything less."

He stopped. There was silence on the film. Then the voice of the interviewer: "I see."

"Jesus Christ," someone said out loud in the dark little theater.

Spiro Agnew's face kept moving in and out of focus.

"Is that the projector or the film?" Garment asked.

The man who had made the films disappeared into the projection booth. The technical quality did not improve.

"Loyalty is the most important principle," Agnew was saying, "when coupled with honesty, that is. And I think that such values are in danger when you hear people advocate violence to change situations which are intolerable . . . and most of the people who are cutting the United States up are doing so without offering a single concrete proposal to improve it."

"How did you become a Republican?" the interviewer asked.

"I became a Republican out of hero worship." Then Spiro

Agnew went on to tell a long story about an old man in the law office where he had first worked as a clerk, and how the old man had been a Republican and how he had admired the old man so much that he had become a Republican, too.

There was more silence on the film. The focus was very bad.

"And . . . and . . . you just sort of went on becoming more and more Republican?"

"That's right," Spiro Agnew said.

More silence. The sailboats moved slowly in the background. The water was very blue. Then the focus made everything a blur.

"What a heartbreak," the man who had made the films said, standing in the back of the theater.

"It looks like you're looking through a Coke bottle," Garment said.

"And he comes across as such an utter bore," Treleaven said. "I don't think the man has had an original observation in his life."

"He is rather nondynamic," Garment said.

Frank Shakespeare was up now and pacing the back of the theater. "We can't use any of this," he said. "That picture quality is awful. Just awful. And Agnew himself, my God. He says all the wrongs things."

"What we need is a shade less truth and a little more pragmatism," Treleaven said.

"I think Dexedrine is the answer," Garment said.

They went to Sardi's for dinner.

"One bright spot," Treleaven said, "you see Agnew and it makes you realize how good Nixon is."

Len Garment was shaking his head. "God, that was awful," he said. "Both Agnew and the questions. Mush meets tapioca. A marriage of meringue."

Then Treleaven left and Shakespeare began to talk about Czechoslovakia and the Russians.

"They're out to get us, Len. They always have been and they always will be. They're ruthless bastards and they're trying to conquer the world. We have to stand up to them at every turn."

"I don't think it's quite that simple," Garment said. "I think maybe some things have changed in twenty years."

"Goddammit, Len, that's just typical of the naive liberal position. I don't see how a man of your intelligence can even consider it. Especially in the face of what's just happened."

"But even there it was different from ten years ago. They didn't murder hundreds of people in the street."

"That's only because the Czechs were taken by surprise. The Russians are just as brutal as they ever were. Look what's happened to Dubcek."

"What's happened to Dubcek?"

"He's been taken somewhere and shot."

"I hadn't heard that."

"Well, they haven't announced it yet, but I'm sure that's what they've done."

"I wouldn't be that positive, Frank."

"You certainly don't think they're going to let him live?"

"They might."

"Oh, Len, the Russians don't work that way. If he's not dead already, I'd be amazed. These are Russians, don't forget. Communists. That's the trouble with this country. Everybody conceives of them as humanitarians, like us. And it's simply not true. They're murderers."

"Then you don't think we've made any progress toward coexistence in twenty years?"

"No, and what's more I don't think any such thing is possible. You can't coexist with men who are trying to enslave you. All that's happened in twenty years is that Americans have allowed themselves to be deceived by the leftist elements of the press."

Shakespeare lived in Greenwich, Connecticut. I was spending the night in Rye, which was on the way.

"I'll drive you home," Shakespeare said, and we walked to the garage near Third Avenue where his car was parked.

"The whole thing about politics," he said, "even at the fringes, is that what you do and say suddenly affects the world. Even in a powerful communications position you can say anything and it really doesn't matter. Nothing changes. But now it's different. Now what we say and do and the way we think makes a difference. Not just for a few people but for the whole nation, the whole world.

"The man we elect President is the leader not just of America but of the western world. The United States is all that stands between the rest of the world and the death of freedom. The Russians cannot be trusted. Americans are naive when it comes to communism. But people recognize, I think, and they're finally starting to care, that Nixon is not as likely to be shoved around by those bastards as HHH. And that's one more reason we're going to win. Because we can get that point, as well as all the others, across to the people through television.

"I'm fatalistic about it," he said, as he drove up the East River Drive. "I believe quite simply that there is a tide of history which will guarantee Nixon's election this year."

"Well, it can't be quite that simple."

"Oh, no. Let me say this. Without television, Richard Nixon would not have a chance. He would not have a prayer of being elected because the press would not let him get through to the people. But because he is so good on television he will get through despite the press. The press doesn't matter anymore.

"We're going to carry New York State, for instance, despite the *Times* and the *Post*. The age of the columnist is over. Television reaches so many more people. You can see it in our attitude toward print advertising. It's used only as a supplement. TV is carrying our campaign. And Nixon loves it. He's overjoyed that he no longer has to depend upon the press.

"It's a more natural relationship anyway, I think. The President has always been hostile to the press. Johnson is the most bitter man in America. He's saying that the press screwed him just because he succeeded Kennedy. He's about ten per cent right. Yet Nixon would be even worse. As President he'd say—in private, of course—'Those liberal bastards are fucking me again.' He has a great hostility toward the press and as President he should be shielded."

Shakespeare drove—a station wagon—through the Bronx.

"How much of the convention did you see on NBC?" he asked.

"Not much. I was there."

"Well, let me tell you about it. It was terrible. Simply dreadful. How about, number one, their using Frank Mankiewicz as a commentator. To cover Nixon yet. And number two, the fact that David Brinkley's wife was one of three hostesses at a reception for newspaper editors' wives at Hickory Hill—the Robert Kennedy home—during the Washington editors' conference."

He paused. There was silence in the car.

"Frank Mankiewicz. I mean that's absurd." Shakespeare said. "Here he had been press secretary to Robert Kennedy. To the man who might very well have been Nixon's opponent. The one Democrat who was probably most diametrically opposed to all that Nixon is and stands for. And he's a commentator on a national network. Supposed to be reporting news.

"And that's not all. It didn't stop there. Do you know that at one point during the convention Mankiewicz made the comment that Nixon was 'half scared to death'?

"Half scared to death. Can you imagine that? And then he compared Nixon to Harold Stassen."

"Does that kind of thing actually bother Nixon?"

"Oh, yes. Absolutely. He's down on NBC. Way down. Of course, RN doesn't know everything that happened. If he did, if he knew how bad they'd really been, he'd be even more upset than he is."

Shakespeare shifted a bit in his seat and began to smile.

"Now. Now listen to this. Here's what I thought I'd do. I thought I'd go to Walter Scott, the NBC board chairman—this would be in private of course, just the two of us in his office—and say, 'Here are the instances. Here are the instances where we feel you've been guilty of bias in your coverage of Nixon. We are going to monitor every minute of your broadcast news, and if this kind of bias continues, and if we are elected, then you just might find yourself in Washington next year answering a few questions. And you just might find yourself having a little trouble getting some of your licenses renewed.' "

Shakespeare paused and smiled. "I'm not going to do it because I'm afraid of the reaction. The press would band together and clobber us. But goddammit, I'd love to."

A few minutes later, reflecting upon his optimism, he said, "We do have one problem. An internal problem. A big one. All these people from the 'sixty and 'sixty-two campaigns are starting to come back. And they say fight. Old style politics.

He hits you, you hit him. These are many of the people who are closest to Nixon, too. I'm fighting them right now. I'm saying that repeated presentation of Nixon as he is will overcome character assassination. But an awful lot of pressure is going to say otherwise. It will be interesting to see what happens. The key to the campaign will be how successfully the candidate resists the advice of the old political types."

We were in Rye.

"Who knows?" Shakespeare was saying. "Agnew might turn out to be another Harry Truman.

"The next thirty days are the most important. Not just for Agnew—for the whole campaign. The images will be formed by October and it will be like putting feathers back into a pillow to change them. Unless RN blows it, and he is not going to do that."

"Yes, but up to now you've had it all your own way. No competition. What happens when Humphrey starts hitting back?"

"Well, we believe they are going to take two tacks. The high road—HHH was always there, for twenty years this is where he's stood, etcetera—and the low road—character assassination: Nixon for President? You can't be serious. He's unprincipled, unstable. Tricky Dick.

"Now, how we answer this is, I think, to a large extent by ignoring it. By continuing to present Nixon as he is today. Calmer, more thoughtful, more compassionate than he was eight years ago. You see, I feel that if he is presented in the proper situations—on television—these qualities will come across. As I said, without television he wouldn't have a chance. With it, he cannot lose."

◄5►

I AM NOT going to barricade myself into a television studio and make this an antiseptic campaign," Richard Nixon said at a press conference a few days after his nomination.

Then he went to Chicago to open his fall campaign. The whole day was built around a television show. Even when ten thousand people stood in front of his hotel and screamed for him to greet them, he stayed locked up in his room, resting for the show.

Chicago was the site of the first ten programs that Nixon would do in states ranging from Massachusetts to Texas. The idea was to have him in the middle of a group of people, answering questions live. Shakespeare and Treleaven had developed the idea through the primaries and now had it sharpened to a point. Each show would run one hour. It would be live to provide suspense; there would be a studio audience to cheer Nixon's answers and make it seem to home viewers that enthusiasm for his candidacy was all but uncontrollable; and there would be an effort to achieve a conversational tone that would penetrate Nixon's stuffiness and drive out the displeasure he often seemed to feel when surrounded by other human beings instead of Bureau of the Budget reports.

One of the valuable things about this idea, from a political standpoint, was that each show would be seen only by the people who lived in that particular state or region. This meant it made no difference if Nixon's statements—for they were not really answers—were exactly the same, phrase for phrase, gesture for gesture, from state to state. Only the press would be bored and the press had been written off already. So Nixon could get through the campaign with a dozen or so carefully worded responses that would cover all the problems of America in 1968.

And, to carry it one step sideways, it made no difference either if the answer varied—in nuance—from state to state. No one, unless he traveled a lot, would hear any statement but the one designed for him. So, a question about law and order might evoke one response in New England and a slightly different one in the South. Nothing big enough to make headlines, just a subtle twist of inflection, or the presence or absence of a frown or gesture as a certain phrase was spoken. This was what the new politics was to Frank Shakespeare. And he did all he could to make sure Richard Nixon's definition would be the same.

Roger Ailes, the executive producer of the Mike Douglas Show, was hired to produce the one-hour programs. Ailes was twenty-eight years old. He had started as a prop boy on the Douglas show in 1965 and was running it within three years. He was good. When he left, Douglas' ratings collapsed. But not everyone he passed on his way up remained his friend. Not even Douglas.

Richard Nixon had been a guest on the show in the fall of 1967. While waiting to go on, he fell into conversation with Roger Ailes.

"It's a shame a man has to use gimmicks like this to get elected," Nixon said.

"Television is not a gimmick," Ailes said.

63

Richard Nixon liked that kind of thinking. He told Len Garment to hire the man.

Ailes had been sent to Chicago three days before Nixon opened the fall campaign. His instructions were to select a panel of questioners and design a set. But now, on the day of the program, only six hours, in fact, before it was to begin, Ailes was having problems.

"Those stupid bastards on the set designing crew put turquoise curtains in the background. Nixon wouldn't look right unless he was carrying a pocketbook." Ailes ordered the curtains removed and three plain, almost stark wooden panels to replace them. "The wood has clean, solid, masculine lines," he said.

His biggest problem was with the panel. Shakespeare, Treleaven and Garment had felt it essential to have a "balanced" group. First, this meant a Negro. One Negro. Not two. Two would be offensive to whites, perhaps to Negroes as well. Two would be trying too hard. One was necessary and safe. Fourteen percent of the population applied to a six- or seven-member panel, equaled one. Texas would be tricky, though. Do you have a Negro *and* a Mexican-American, or if not, then which?

Besides the Negro, the panel for the first show included a Jewish attorney, the president of a Polish-Hungarian group, a suburban housewife, a businessman, a representative of the white lower middle class, and, for authenticity, two newsmen: one from Chicago, one from Moline.

That was all right, Roger Ailes said. But then someone had called from New York and insisted that he add a farmer. A farmer, for Christ's sake. Roger Ailes had been born in Ohio, but even so he knew you did not want a farmer on a television show. All they did was ask complicated questions about things like parities, which nobody else understood or cared about. Including Richard Nixon. He would appoint a secretary of agriculture when he won, yes, but why did he have to talk to farmers on live television in the campaign?

Besides, the farmer brought the panel size to eight, which Ailes said was too big. It would be impossible for Nixon to establish interpersonal relationships with eight different people in one hour. And interpersonal relationships were the key to success.

"This is the trouble with all these political people horning in," Ailes said. "Fine, they all get their lousy little groups represented but we wind up with a horseshit show."

There was to be a studio audience—three hundred people —recruited by the local Republican organization. Just enough Negroes so the press could not write "all-white" stories but not enough so it would look like a ballpark. The audience, of course, would applaud every answer Richard Nixon gave, boosting his confidence and giving the impression to a viewer that Nixon certainly did have charisma, and whatever other qualities he wanted his President to have.

Treleaven and his assistant, Al Scott, came to the studio late in the afternoon. They were getting nervous. "Nixon's throat is scratchy," Treleaven said, "and that's making him upset." Al Scott did not like the lighting in the studio.

"The lights are too high," he said. "They'll show the bags under RN's eyes."

Then there was a crisis about whether the press should be allowed in the studio during the show. Shakespeare had given an order that they be kept out. Now they were complaining to Herb Klein, the press relations man, that if three hundred shills could be bussed in to cheer, a pool of two or three reporters could be allowed to sit in the stands.

Shakespeare still said no. No *newspapermen* were going to interfere with his TV show. Klein kept arguing, saying that if this was how it was going to start, on the very first day of the campaign, it was going to be 1960 again within a week.

Treleaven and Ailes went upstairs, to the WBBM cafeteria, and drank vending machine coffee from paper cups.

"I agree with Frank," Ailes said. "Fuck 'em. It's not a press conference."

"But if you let the audience in . . ."

"Doesn't matter. The audience is part of the show. And that's the whole point. It's a television show. Our television show. And the press has no business on the set. And goddammit, Harry, the problem is that this is an electronic election. The first there's ever been. TV has the power now. Some of the guys get arrogant and rub the reporters' faces in it and then the reporters get pissed and go out of their way to rap anything they consider staged for TV. And you know damn well that's what they'd do if they saw this from the studio. You let them in with the regular audience and they see the warmup. They see Jack Rourke out there telling the audience to applaud and to mob Nixon at the end, and that's all they'd write about. You know damn well it is." Jack Rourke was Roger Ailes's assistant.

"I'm still afraid we'll create a big incident if we lock them out entirely," Treleaven said. "I'm going to call Frank and suggest he reconsider."

But Shakespeare would not. He arranged for monitors in an adjacent studio and said the press could watch from there, seeing no more, no less, than what they would see from any living room in Illinois.

It was five o'clock now; the show was to start at nine. Ray Voege, the makeup man, borrowed from the Johnny Carson Show, had arrived.

"Oh, Ray," Roger Ailes said, "with Wilkinson, watch that perspiration problem on the top of his forehead."

"Yes, he went a little red in Portland," Ray Voege said.

"And when he's off camera, I'd give him a treated towel, just like Mr. Nixon uses."

"Right."

Ailes turned to Jack Rourke, the assistant. "Also, I'd like to have Wilkinson in the room with Nixon before the show to kibitz around, get Nixon loose."

"Okay, I'll bring him in."

Then Treleaven and Scott went back to the Sheraton Hotel for dinner. Ailes stayed in the studio to rehearse the opening with the cameramen one more time. There was nothing he could do about what Nixon would say or would not say, but he did not want anyone turning off before the hour was over because the program was dull to watch.

The set, now that it was finished, was impressive. There was a round blue-carpeted platform, six feet in diameter and eight inches high. Richard Nixon would stand on this and face the panel, which would be seated in a semicircle around him. Bleachers for the audience ranged out behind the panel chairs. Later, Roger Ailes would think to call the whole effect, "the arena concept" and bill Nixon as "the man in the arena." He got this from a Theodore Roosevelt quote which hung, framed, from a wall of his office in Philadelphia. It said something about how one man in the arena was worth ten, or a hundred, or a thousand carping critics.

At nine o'clock, Central Daylight Time, Richard Nixon, freshly powdered, left his dressing room, walked down a corridor deserted save for secret service, and went through a carefully guarded doorway that opened onto the rear of the set.

Harry Treleaven had selected tape from WBBM's coverage of the noontime motorcade for the opening of the show. Tape that showed Richard Nixon riding, arms outstretched, beaming, atop an open car. Hundreds of thousands of citizens, some who had come on their own, some who had been recruited by Republican organizations, cheered, waved balloons and tossed confetti in the air. One week before, at the Democratic convention, it had been Humphrey, blood, and tear gas. Today it was Nixon, the unifying hero, the man to heal all wounds. No disorder in his crowds, just dignified Republican enthusiasm, heightened a notch or two by knowledge of the inevitable comparisons between this event and those of the previous week. If the whole world had been watching then, at least a fair portion would see this on the network news. Chicago Republicans showed a warm, assured, united front. And Harry Treleaven picked only the most magical of moments for the opening of his show.

Then the director hit a button and Bud Wilkinson appeared on the screen. And what a placid, composed, substantial, reassuring figure he was: introducing his close personal friend, a man whose intelligence and judgment had won the respect of the world's leaders and the admiration of millions of his countrymen, this very same man who had been seen entering Jerusalem moments ago on tape: Richard Nixon.

And the carefully cued audience (for Jack Rourke, the warmup man, had done his job well) stood to render an ovation. Richard Nixon, grinning, waving, *thrusting*, walked to the blue riser to receive the tribute.

It was warmly given. Genuine. For Nixon suddenly represented a true alternative: peace, prosperity, an end to discord, a return to the stable values that had come under such rude and unwarranted attack. Nixon was fortification, reaffirmation of much that needed to be reaffirmed. They needed him now, these Republicans, much more than they had in 1960. Then they were smug; and they did not especially like him. They toyed with him, as a small boy would poke a frog

68

with a stick. They made him suffer needlessly, and, in the end, their apathy had dragged a nation down. Now, on this night, this first night of his campaign to restore decency and honor to American life, they wanted to let him know they cared. To let him know 1960 would not happen again.

He looked toward his wife; the two daughters; Ed Brooke, the most useful Negro he had found; Charles Percy, the organization man; and Thruston Morton, resigned if not enthusiastic. They sat in the first row together.

Then, eagerly, forcefully, strong, confident, alive, he turned toward the panel to begin.

He was alone, with not even a chair on the platform for company; ready to face, if not the nation, at least Illinois. To communicate, man to man, eye to eye, with that mass of the ordinary whose concerns he so deeply shared; whose values were so totally his own. All the subliminal effects sank in. Nixon stood alone, ringed by forces which, if not hostile, were at least—to the viewer—unpredictable.

There was a rush of sympathy; a desire—a need, even—to root. Richard Nixon was suddenly human: facing a new and dangerous situation, alone, armed only with his wits. In image terms, he had won before he began. All the old concepts had been destroyed. He had achieved a new level of communication. The stronger his statement, the stronger the surge of warmth inside the viewer. *Received impressions.* Yes, this was a man who could lead; infinitely preferable to the gray and bumbling Johnson; the inscrutable, unsuccessful Rusk. A man who—yes, they remembered, even through the electronic haze—had stood up to Khrushchev in the kitchen. And, it was obvious now, who would stand up to Jerry Rubin in the street.

His statements flowed like warm milk, bathed the audience, restored faith in the Founding Fathers, rekindled the memory of a vigorous Eisenhower, of ten, of fifteen years before. *"The American Revolution has been won,"* he had said in his acceptance speech at Miami, *"the American Dream has come true."*

Morris Liebman, the Jewish attorney, asked the first question: "Would you comment on the accusation which was made from time to time that your views have shifted and that they are based on expediences?"

Richard Nixon squinted and smiled. "I suppose what you are referring to is: Is there a new Nixon or is there an old Nixon? I suppose I could counter by saying: Which Humphrey shall we listen to today?"

There was great applause for this. When it faded, Richard Nixon said, "I do want to say this: There certainly is a new Nixon. I realize, too, that as a man gets older he learns something. If I haven't learned something I am not worth anything in public life.

"We live in a new world. Half the nations in the world were born since World War Two. Half the people living in the world today were born since World War Two. The problems are different and I think I have had the good sense—I trust the intelligence—to travel the world since I left the office of Vice President and to bring my views up to date to deal with the new world.

"I think my principles are consistent. I believe very deeply in the American system. I believe very deeply in what is needed to defend that system at home and abroad. I think I have some ideas as to how we can promote peace, ideas that are different from what they were eight years ago, not because I have changed but because the problems have changed.

"My answer is, yes, there is a new Nixon, if you are talking in terms of new ideas for the new world and the America we live in. In terms of what I believe in the American view and the American dream, I think I am just what I was eight years ago."

Applause swept the studio. Bud Wilkinson joined in.

The farmer asked a question about farming; the Polish-Hungarian delivered an address concerning the problems of the people of eastern Europe. His remarks led to no question at all, but no matter: Richard Nixon expressed concern for the plight of eastern Europeans everywhere, including northern Illinois.

Then Warner Saunders, the Negro, and a very acceptable, very polite one he seemed to be, asked, "What does law and order mean to you?"

"I am quite aware," Richard Nixon said, "of the fact that the black community, when they hear it, think of power being used in a way that is destructive to them, and yet I think we have to also remember that the black community as well as the white community has an interest in order and in law, providing that law is with justice. To me law and order must be combined with justice. Now that's what I want for America. I want the kind of law and order which deserves respect."

John McCarter, the businessman, asked about Spiro Agnew. Nixon said, "Of all the men who I considered, Spiro Agnew had the intelligence, the courage and the principle to take on the great responsibilities of a campaigner and responsibilities of Vice President. And who also had the judgment so that if anything happened, the President of the United States could sit in that chair and make decisions that need to be made that would make the difference between war and peace and that I would have confidence in him." Then he called Agnew "a man of compassion."

McCarter came back later wanting to know if Nixon

thought the Chicago police had been too harsh on demonstrators in the streets.

"It would be easy," Nixon said, "to criticize Mayor Daley and by implication Vice President Humphrey. But it wouldn't be right for me to lob in criticism. I am not going to get into it. It is best for political figures not to be making partisan comments from the sidelines."

The show went on like that. At the end the audience charged from the bleachers, as instructed. They swarmed around Richard Nixon so that the last thing the viewer at home saw was Nixon in the middle of this big crowd of people, who all thought he was great.

Treleaven plunged into the crowd. He was excited; he thought the show had been brilliant. He got to Nixon just as Nixon was bending down to autograph a cast that a girl was wearing on her leg.

"Well, you've got a leg up," Treleaven said.

Nixon stood up and grinned and moved away.

"Gee, that was sure a funny look he gave me," Treleaven said. "I wonder if he heard me. I wonder if he knew who I was."

Three days later, Roger Ailes composed a memorandum that contained the details of his reaction to the show. He sent it to Shakespeare and Garment:

After completing the first one-hour program, I thought I would put a few general comments down on paper. After you have had a chance to look them over, I'd like to discuss them briefly with you so we can steadily improve the programs up to the time he becomes President. I viewed the complete tape the morning after the show.

Mr. Nixon is strong now on television and has good control of the situation.

I.   The Look:

A. He looks good on his feet and shooting "in the round" gives dimension to him.

B. Standing adds to his "feel" of confidence and the viewers' "feel" of his confidence.

C. He still uses his arms a little too "predictably" and a little too often, but at this point it is better not to inhibit him.

D. He seems to be comfortable on his feet and even appears graceful and relaxed, i.e., hands on his hips or arms folded occasionally.

E. His eye contact is good with the panelists, but he should play a little more to the home audience via the head-on camera. I would like to talk to him about this.

F. We are still working on lightening up his eyes a bit, but this is not a major problem. This will be somewhat tougher in smaller studios, but don't worry, he will never look bad:

    1. I may lower the front two key spots a bit.

    2. I may try slightly whiter makeup on upper eyelids.

    3. I may lower the riser he stands on a couple of inches.

G. The "arena" effect is excellent and he plays to all areas well. The look has "guts."

H. Color lights are hot and he has a tendency to perspire, especially along the upper lip.

    1. Whenever he is going to tape a show, the studio air conditioning should be turned up full at least four hours prior to broadcast, and camera rehearsal should be limited as much as possible in this time period to keep the lights off and the heat down. If camera rehearsal is necessary, the air conditioner should be turned on sooner and the studio sealed off. Keep all studio doors (especially the large leading doors) closed.

I. An effort should be made to keep him in the sun occasionally to maintain a fairly constant level of healthy tan.

J. Generally, he has a very "Presidential" look and style—he smiles easily (and looks good doing it). He should continue to make lighter comments once in a while for pacing.

II. The Questions and Answers:

A. First, his opening remarks are good. He should, perhaps, be prepared with an optional cut in his closing remarks in case we get into time trouble getting off the air. I don't want to take a chance of missing the shots of the audience crowding around him at the end. Bud can specifically tell him exactly how much time he has to close.

B. In the panel briefing we should tell the panelists not to ask two-part questions. This slows down the overall pace of the show and makes it difficult for the viewer to remember and thus follow. Instead, the panelists should be instructed that they can continue a dialogue with Mr. Nixon—ask two questions in a row to get the answers.

C. Some of the answers are still too long and over half tended to be the same length. Nixon in Illinois Answers:

1. Approximately 3:00
2. 1:45
3. 1:30
4. 2:33—agriculture
5. 1:30—education
6. 2:37—European question, Dr. Ripa
   —Question was longer than answer.
7. 2:09—law & order
8. 3:22—Justice Earl Warren
9. 2:15—foreign aid
10. 3:00—NATO aid
11. 2:23—police in Chicago
    —(What he really said was that he had no comment.)
12. 2:30—urban renewal
13. :25—detention camps
    —(Excellent answer—He didn't know but he was honest and the audience was with him completely.)
14. :53
15. 2:45—income tax
16. 2:15—priority of spending

17. 1:47—money
18. :25—Vietnam POWs
19. :49—David & Julie
20. Wrap-up—perfect at :58.

—On one answer from Warner Saunders, he gave an unqualified "yes" and that was good. Whenever possible he should be that definite.

D. He still needs some memorable phrases to use in wrapping up certain points. I feel that I might be able to help in this area, but don't know if you want me to or if he would take suggestions from me on this. Maybe I could have a session with Price and Buchanan.

III. Staging:

A. The microphone cord needs to be dressed and looped to the side.

B. Bud Wilkinson felt there should be more women on the panel since over half the voters are women. Maybe combine a category, i.e., woman reporter or negro woman.

C. The panel was too large at eight. Maximum should be seven, six is still preferable to give more interaction.

D. Bud should be able to interject more often with some prepared lighter or pacing questions.

E. The family should be in the audience at every show. Should I talk with them, Whitaker, or will you?

F. Political VIPs should be in the audience for every show. Nixon handles these introductions extremely well and they are good for reaction shots.

G. I am adding extenders to the zoom lens on all cameras to allow closer shooting for reactions.

IV. General:

A. The show got off to a slow start. Perhaps the opening could be made more exciting by:
    1. adding music or applause earlier.

B. The excitement of the film made the quietness of the dissolve to the studio more apparent.

C. Bud should be introduced with applause.

D. When film is not available it might be good to have David Douglas Duncan shoot a series of interesting stills which could be put on film and synchronized to the Connie Francis record. I'd like to try this—it might give us a classy "standard" opening to use.

E. To give the director as much advantage as possible—the fewer last-minute changes, the better. In Chicago we luckily had excellent facilities and a fast crew plus plenty of rehearsal time. In the California show, because of studio priorities, our rehearsal time is cut in half.

F. I will work with the director on the art of using the reaction shot for better overall program value.

G. In general, I usually feel "down" immediately after taping a show. I was more pleased after viewing the tape than I was that night after the show.

◄6►

WITH ALL OF Fuller and Smith and Ross to choose from, when Harry Treleaven did need help, he wound up hiring Len Garment's brother.

Charley Garment was a methodical little man with a beard who had been producer of the Monitor show on NBC radio. In the beginning he said he was willing to work for Nixon but he did not want his name connected with it. This was common: Charley Garment, Gene Jones, Paul Keyes from Laugh-In, all these people who said they wanted to help *as long as their names weren't involved.*

Charley Garment came to supervise a series of endorsements that Treleaven wanted to tape. There were two kinds: political and celebrity. The list of political names was much the longer of the two. A President could do more to a congressman who said no than to a singer. In fact, the day Charley Garment started, the only names on the celebrity list were Art Linkletter, Connie Francis, Pat Boone, John Wayne, and Lawrence Welk. And it turned out Welk didn't want his name used, either.

The first job Charley Garment was given was to film a commercial with Connie Francis.

"I don't know whether it's better to have her come on straight or open up with a scene of her listening to the end of her own recording of the Nixon jingle," Charley Garment was saying. "Then we could have the announcer come out and say, 'Well, Connie, we know you like Richard Nixon. How about telling us why?' And then she could go into it."

"I think that's too obvious," Treleaven said. "It looks too much like a commercial."

"But, Harry, the problem is this is to be a sixty-second spot and talking, I don't know how long she's good for. I think we can only get about thirty seconds out of her. She might be good for the minute but I doubt it."

"I'm not sure the other is a good idea, though, Charley."

"But she only has a short message. We should have her give it and bang! get her out of there. Besides, I don't think the audience minds the commercial approach. We've spent billions of dollars making them accept it and now they do. They're conditioned."

Connie Francis once had been very popular with those records where her voice was recorded on several different tracks and then all the tracks were played together so she sounded like the McGuire Sisters. Later, when that novelty wore off, she began to make records of Italian songs. Much later, when even the Italian songs were not getting played much on the radio, she started to show up at places like the Merv Griffin Show where she would tell how proud she was of what America was doing in Vietnam and how disgusting it was to see men without crew cuts.

"Look," Treleaven said, "the first day Len and Frank told me about her, do you know what I said? I said, 'Who's Connie Francis?' And they said, 'Who's Connie Francis? You must be kidding. She's the biggest thing around.'"

Then Treleaven shook his head. "I really must stay more current."

The commercial ran on the Laugh-In show in September.

The next day, in the *Times*, Jack Gould wrote that it "embraced all the ills of the oversimplified campaign spot announcement. Connie Francis . . . said that in her overseas travels she found disrespect for the United States, and here at home there was a regrettable lack of respect for authority. Mr. Nixon, she said, would put matters aright if elected. Admittedly, it is a forlorn hope but one could wish that the supporters of Mr. Nixon, Vice President Humphrey and Mr. Wallace would keep tawdry advertising pitches out of the business of choosing a President."

"I'm really learning to hate that girl," Treleaven said.

The political endorsements went more smoothly. The only serious problem was with John Lindsay. He had given a seconding speech for Spiro Agnew in Miami and apparently had been having trouble digesting his food ever since. The day Charley Garment and the film crew walked in to get his endorsement the first thing they heard was that he was not going to endorse anybody, goddammit, particularly Richard Nixon, unless someone strangled Agnew.

Charley Garment was shaken. "The mayor blew his stack in a most undignified manner," he reported to Treleaven the next morning. "He attacked us for all the ills of the world." Then Charley Garment shook his head slowly from side to side. "I'm glad he's not the candidate, I really am. I wouldn't want his finger on the button."

The Lindsay endorsement was never used. Treleaven said it was "lukewarm" and he did not think it would be very effective.

It was about this time that the results of the Semantic Differential Test came in. Treleaven and Garment and Shakespeare went into the big meeting room at Fuller and

Smith and Ross and watched a tall, thin, frowning man named John Maddox explain what all of it meant.

"The semantic differential is the most sensitive instrument known to modern marketing research," he said. Then he pointed to a big chart on a slide screen on the wall. Running down the chart were twenty-six pairs of adjectives or phrases such as weak–strong, wishy-washy–firm, stuffed shirt–sense of humor, tense–relaxed, stingy–generous, and on like that. The bad description, like wishy-washy or stingy was on the left side of the chart, the good one on the right. In between were the numbers one through seven.

John Maddox explained that he had gone all through the country asking people to evaluate the presidential candidates on the scale of one through seven, and also asking them to evaluate the qualities an ideal President would have. If they thought Humphrey, for instance, was very generous they would give him a seven on the stingy–generous line; if they thought he was not much of either they would give him a three or a four. Maddox had plotted what he called the Ideal President Curve, which was the line connecting the points that represented the average rating in each category as applied to the ideal. Then Maddox plotted curves for Nixon, Humphrey and Wallace. The gaps between the Nixon line and the Ideal line represented the personality traits that Nixon should try to improve. It was considered especially important, Maddox said, that Nixon close the "Personality Gap" between himself and Humphrey.

"It is of substantial significance, we believe," Maddox wrote later in a report, "that the widest gap of all is the 'cold–warm.' We believe it highly probable that if the real personal warmth of Mr. Nixon could be more adequately exposed, it would release a flood of other inhibitions about him

—and make him more tangible as a person to large numbers of Humphrey leaners."

Maddox had other charts which broke the responses down geographically and ethnically so people could see what kind of personality gap existed in the minds of southern Negroes or midwestern whites. The idea was, even if Nixon would not start to act warmer, Harry Treleaven could produce commercials that would make him seem so.

But now, in September, the campaign was starting to drift out of Harry Treleaven's control. Nixon had never liked the idea of advertising men giving him an image, and now that he had the image he wanted to get rid of the men. As Shakespeare had feared, Nixon's old friends had pushed their way back to his side and with them now were the new men who thought like old friends: 1950s-type friends. Men who thought Marshall McLuhan starred in *Gunsmoke*.

John Mitchell was the campaign manager. R. W. Haldeman was chief of staff. They were telling Richard Nixon everything that Shakespeare and Treleaven did not want him to hear. They told him he did not need television. That if he only would play it safe, wiggle his fingers, say "sock it to 'em" at every stop and use law and order six times in each speech there was no way he could lose. And Richard Nixon, who is a cautious man, listened. What they told him was what he wanted to hear. Treleaven, Shakespeare, and Garment had done good work, but they made him uneasy.

Six months earlier, Nixon had said, "We're going to build this whole campaign around television. You fellows just tell me what you want me to do and I'll do it." Now he was grumbling about a one-hour taping session once a week.

"They're really out of the woodwork," Treleaven said. "In March, when it was a long, uphill struggle, nobody cared what commercials we used. Now we have a screening and John Mitchell shows up with six guys I don't even know."

There was something very wrong in this, Treleaven felt. Something very wrong about politicians interfering with a political campaign. Especially one that Harry Treleaven had planned so well.

The problem was that Richard Nixon really was the 1950s. The Bud Wilkinson bit was not just an act. Richard Nixon did not trust television. He refused to look at himself, even on a newscast. He refused to use a teleprompter, no matter how long his speech. Television was just one more slick eastern trick and he was a poor boy from the West.

So Nixon began to pull back. The desperation he had felt in early spring was gone. He was leading now. He was going to win. He would continue to run a television campaign, yes; it was the easiest way to dodge the press. But he would do it his way from now on. And that meant that no matter how many technical tricks Frank Shakespeare or Roger Ailes tried to teach him, he would show them he could be just as dull and artificial on television as he had ever been in person.

◄7►

ONE DAY Harry Treleaven came into his office with two reels of movie film under his arm.

"Come on," he said. "I think you'd like to see this." We went into the big meeting room and he gave the film to a man in the projection booth.

The film was in black and white. There was a title: *A Face of War*. It had been made in Vietnam. It was the story of three months of fighting done by a single infantry platoon. There was no music or narration. Just the faces and sounds of jungle war.

Halfway through the first reel, Len Garment and Frank Shakespeare came in. They were there for a one o'clock meeting. They took seats and began to watch the film. Neither spoke. They watched the men crawling single file through the jungle, heard the sound the leaves made as they brushed the faces of the men and heard the sound of rain and bullets and mortar shells in the night. The reel ended. The meeting was due to begin. Harry Treleaven turned to the projection booth. "Play the second reel," he said. Ruth Jones came in for the meeting and watched the film for three minutes and left. "I can't sit through that," she said.

No one else spoke. There were only the men trying to kill and trying to avoid being killed in the jungle.

Twenty minutes later, with the film still running, Art Duram said, "Don't you think we'd better start?" No one moved or gave any sign of having heard.

"It's half past one already."

Harry Treleaven sat up in his chair and looked at his watch. "All right, that's enough," he said to the man in the projection booth.

The lights came on in the room. No one spoke for a moment. Each man was still staring at where the film had been.

"That's the most powerful thing I've ever seen," Len Garment said.

"What is it?" Frank Shakespeare said.

Harry Treleaven stood and stepped toward the projection booth. "It's called *A Face of War*," he said, "and it was made by the man I want to hire to do our spot commercials."

Originally, Treleaven had wanted David Douglas Duncan, the photographer, to make commercials. Duncan was a friend of Richard Nixon's but when Treleaven took him out to lunch he said no, he would be too busy. Then Duncan mentioned Eugene Jones.

Treleaven had wanted Duncan because he had decided to make still photography the basis of Richard Nixon's sixty-second television commercial campaign. He had learned a little about stills at J. Walter Thompson when he used them for some Pan American spots. Now he thought they were the perfect thing for Nixon because Nixon himself would not have to appear.

Treleaven could use Nixon's voice to accompany the stills but his face would not be on the screen. Instead there would be pictures, and hopefully, the pictures would prevent people from paying too much attention to the words.

The words would be the same ones Nixon always used—the words of the acceptance speech. But they would all seem fresh and lively because a series of still pictures would flash on the screen while Nixon spoke. If it were done right, it would permit Treleaven to create a Nixon image that was entirely independent of the words. Nixon would say his same old tiresome things but no one would have to listen. The words would become Muzak. Something pleasant and lulling in the background. The flashing pictures would be carefully selected to create the impression that somehow Nixon represented competence, respect for tradition, serenity, faith that the American people were better than people anywhere else, and that all these problems others shouted about meant nothing in a land blessed with the tallest buildings, strongest armies, biggest factories, cutest children, and rosiest sunsets in the world. Even better: through association with the pictures, Richard Nixon could *become* these very things.

Obviously, some technical skill would be required. David Douglas Duncan said Gene Jones was the man.

Treleaven met Jones and was impressed. "He's low-key," Treleaven said. "He doesn't come at you as a know-it-all."

Gene Jones, also in his middle forties, had been taking movies of wars half his life. He did it perhaps as well as any man ever has. Besides that, he had produced the Today show on NBC for eight years and had done a documentary series on famous people called *The World of* . . . Billy Graham, Sophia Loren, anyone who had been famous and was willing to be surrounded by Jones's cameras for a month.

Jones understood perfectly what Treleaven was after. A technique through which Richard Nixon would seem to be contemporary, imaginative, involved—without having to say anything of substance. Jones had never done commercial work before but for $110,000, from which he would pay salaries to a nine-man staff, he said he would do it for Nixon.

"A hundred and ten thousand dollars," Frank Shakespeare said after seeing *A Face of War*. "That's pretty steep."

"I wouldn't know," Treleaven said. "I have nothing to compare it to."

"It's pretty steep."

"He's pretty good."

"Yes, he is."

"What do you think?"

"Oh, I have no objection. That just hit me as a very high price."

"I'd like approval to pay it right now. I want to hire him immediately."

"Fine," Frank Shakespeare said. "You've got it."

A day or two later Jones came down to Treleaven's office to discuss details such as where he should set up a studio and what areas the first set of spots should cover.

"This will not be a commercial sell," Jones said. "It will not have the feel of something a—pardon the expression—an agency would turn out. I see it as sort of a miniature *Project 20*. And I can't see anyone turning it off a television set, quite frankly."

That same day Jones rented two floors of the building at 303 East Fifty-third Street, one flight up from a nightclub called Chuck's Composite. Within three days, he had his staff at work. Buying pictures, taking pictures, taking motion pictures of still pictures that Jones himself had cropped and arranged in a sequence.

"I'm pretty excited about this," Jones said. "I think we can give it an artistic dimension."

Harry Treleaven did not get excited about anything but he was at least intrigued by this. "It will be interesting to see how he translates his approach into political usefulness," Treleaven said.

"Yes," Frank Shakespeare said, "if he can."

Gene Jones would start work at five o'clock in the morning. Laying coffee and doughnuts on his desk, he would spread a hundred or so pictures on the floor, taken from boxes into which his staff already had filed them. The boxes had labels like VIETNAM . . . DEMOCRATIC CONVENTION . . . POVERTY: HARLEM, CITY SLUMS, GHETTOS . . . FACES; HAPPY AMERICAN PEOPLE AT WORK AND LEISURE . . .

He would select a category to fit the first line of whatever script he happened to be working with that day. The script would contain the words of Richard Nixon. Often they would be exactly the words he had used in the acceptance speech, but re-recorded in a hotel room somewhere so the tone would be better suited to commercial use.

Jones would select the most appropriate of the pictures and then arrange and rearrange, as in a game of solitaire. When he had the effect he thought he wanted he would work with a stopwatch and red pencil, marking each picture on the back to indicate what sort of angle and distance the movie camera should shoot from and how long it should linger on each still.

"The secret is in juxtaposition," Jones said. "The relationships, the arrangement. After twenty-five years, the other things—the framing and the panning, are easy."

Everyone was excited about the technique and the way it could be used to make people feel that Richard Nixon belonged in the White House. The only person who was not impressed was Nixon. He was in a hotel room in San Francisco one day, recording the words for one of the early commercials. The machine was turned on before Nixon realized it and the end of his conversation was picked up.

"I'm not sure I like this kind of a . . . of a format, incidentally," Nixon said. "Ah . . . I've seen these kinds of things and I don't think they're very . . . very effective. . . ."

Still, Nixon read the words he had been told to read:

"In recent years crime in this country has grown nine times as fast as the population. At the current rate, the crimes of violence in America will double by nineteen seventy-two. We cannot accept that kind of future. We owe it to the decent and law-abiding citizens of America to take the offensive against the criminal forces that threaten their peace and security and to rebuild respect for law across this country. I pledge to you that the wave of crime is not going to be the wave of the future in America."

There was nothing new in these words. Harry Treleaven had simply paraphrased and condensed the standard law and order message Nixon had been preaching since New Hampshire. But when the words were coupled with quickly flashing colored pictures of criminals, of policemen patrolling deserted streets, of bars on storefront windows, of disorder on a college campus, of peace demonstrators being led bleeding into a police van, then the words became something more than what they actually were. It was the whole being greater than the sum of its parts.

In the afternoons, Treleaven, Garment and Shakespeare would go to Gene Jones' studio to look at the films on a little machine called a movieola. If they were approved, Jones would take them to a sound studio down the street to blend in music, but they never were approved right away. There was not one film that Garment or Shakespeare did not order changed for a "political" reason. Anything that might offend Strom Thurmond, that might annoy the Wallace voter whom Nixon was trying so hard for; any ethnic nuance that Jones, in his preoccupation with artistic viewpoint, might have missed: these came out.

"Gene is good," Treleaven explained, "but he needs a lot of political guidance. He doesn't always seem to be aware of the point we're trying to make."

Jones didn't like the changes. "I'm not an apprentice," he said. "I'm an experienced pro and never before in my career have I had anyone stand over my shoulder telling me to change this and change that. It might sound like bullshit, but when you pull out a shot or two it destroys the dynamism, the whole flow."

The first spot was called simply *Vietnam*. Gene Jones had been there for ninety days, under fire, watching men kill and die, and he had been wounded in the neck himself. Out of the experience had come *A Face of War*. And out of it now came E.S.J. [for Eugene S. Jones] #1, designed to help Richard Nixon become President. Created for no other purpose.

VIDEO	AUDIO
1. OPENING NETWORK DIS-CLAIMER: "A POLITICAL ANNOUNCEMENT."	
2. FADEUP ON FAST PACED SCENES OF HELO AS-SAULT IN VIETNAM.	SFX AND UNDER

VIDEO

3. WOUNDED AMERICANS AND VIETNAMESE.

4. MONTAGE OF FACIAL CU's OF AMERICAN SERVICEMEN AND VIETNAMESE NATIVES WITH QUESTIONING, ANXIOUS, PERPLEXED ATTITUDE.

5. PROUD FACES OF VIETNAMESE PEASANTS ENDING IN CU OF THE WORD "LOVE" SCRAWLED ON THE HELMET OF AMERICAN G.I. AND PULL BACK TO REVEAL HIS FACE.

AUDIO

R.N.

Never has so much military, economic, and diplomatic power been used as ineffectively as in Vietnam.

And if after all of this time and all of this sacrifice and all of this support there is still no end in sight, then I say the time has come for the American people to turn to new leadership—not tied to the policies and mistakes of the past.

I pledge to you: we will have an honorable end to the war in Vietnam.

MUSIC UP AND OUT.

Harry Treleaven and Len Garment and Frank Shakespeare thought this commercial was splendid.

"Wow, that's powerful," Treleaven said.

Dead soldiers and empty words. The war was not bad because of insane suffering and death. The war was bad because it was *ineffective*.

So Richard Nixon, in his commercial, talked about new leadership for the war. New leadership like Ellsworth Bunker and Henry Cabot Lodge and U. Alexis Johnson.

Vietnam was shown across the country for the first time on September 18. Jack Gould did not like this one any more than he had liked Connie Francis.

"The advertising agency working in behalf of Richard Nixon unveiled another unattractive campaign spot announcement," he wrote. "Scenes of wounded GIs were the visual complement for Mr. Nixon's view that he is better equipped to handle the agony of the Vietnamese war. Rudimentary good taste in politics apparently is automatically ruled out when Madison Avenue gets into the act."

The fallen soldiers bothered other people in other ways. There was on the Nixon staff an "ethnic specialist" named Kevin Phillips, whose job it was to determine what specific appeals would work with specific nationalities and in specific parts of the country. He watched *Vietnam* and sent a quick and alarmed memo to Len Garment: "This has a decidedly dovish impact as a result of the visual content and it does not seem suitable for use in the South and Southwest."

His reasoning was quite simple. A picture of a wounded soldier was a reminder that the people who fight wars get hurt. This, he felt, might cause resentment among those Americans who got such a big kick out of cheering for wars from their Legion halls and barrooms half a world away. So bury the dead in silence, Kevin Phillips said, before you blow North Carolina.

Another problem arose in the Midwest: annoyance over the word "Love" written on the soldier's helmet.

"It reminds them of hippies," Harry Treleaven said. "We've gotten several calls already from congressmen complaining. They don't think it's the sort of thing soldiers should be writing on their helmets."

Len Garment ordered the picture taken out of the commercial. Gene Jones inserted another at the end; this time a soldier whose helmet was plain.

This was the first big case of "political" guidance, and for a full week the more sensitive members of the Gene Jones staff mourned the loss of their picture.

"It was such a beautiful touch," one of them said. "And we

thought, what an interesting young man it must be who would write 'Love' on his helmet even as he went into combat."

Then E.S.J. Productions received a letter from the mother of the soldier. She told what a thrill it had been to see her son's picture in one of Mr. Nixon's commercials, and she asked if there were some way that she might obtain a copy of the photograph.

The letter was signed: Mrs. William Love.

Almost all the commercials ran sixty seconds. But Jones did one, called E.S.J. #3: *Look at America,* that went more than four minutes.

VIDEO	AUDIO
2. FADEUP ON FAST, DRA-MATIC RIOT IN CITY, FLAMING BUILDINGS.	ELECTRONIC MUSIC UP FULL.
3. VIETNAM COMBAT.	ELECTRONIC MUSIC CONTINUES AND UNDER.
4. G.I. IN VIETNAM SLUMPS DEJECTEDLY.	R.N. America is in trouble today not because her people have failed, but because her leaders have failed. Let us look at America. Let us listen to America. We see Americans dying on distant battlefields abroad.
5. RIOT & FIRES.	We see Americans hating each other; fighting each other; killing each other at home.

VIDEO   AUDIO

We see cities enveloped in smoke and flame.

6. FIRE ENGINES.   We hear sirens in the night.

7. PERPLEXED FACES OF   As we see and hear these things,
   AMERICANS.   millions of Americans cry out in
                                      anguish.

                                      Did we come all the way for this?

8. MONTAGE URBAN & RU-   MUSIC UP AND UNDER.
   RAL DECAY—(hungry in
   Appalachia-poor in ghetto-ill-
   clothed on Indian reserva-
   tions. Unemployment in cities
   and welfare in small towns).

9. MONTAGE OF AMERI-   R.N.
   CANS "CREATING AND   Let us listen now to another
   CONTRIBUTING" MOTI-   voice. It is the voice of the great
   VATES INTO CU's OF   majority of Americans—the non-
   FACES.   shouters; the non-demonstrators.

                                      They are not racists or sick; they
                                      are not guilty of the crime that
                                      plagues the land.

                                      They are black and they are
                                      white—native born and foreign
                                      born—young and old.

                                      They work in America's factories.

                                      They run American business.

                                      They serve in government.

                                      They provide most of the soldiers
                                      who died to keep us free.

VIDEO

AUDIO

CONTINUING MONTAGE
OF "CREATIVE & CON-
TRIBUTING FACES."

They give drive to the spirit of
America.

They give lift to the American
Dream.

They give steel to the back-bone
of America.

They are good people, decent
people; they work, they save, they
pay their taxes, they care. Like
Theodore Roosevelt, they know
that this country will not be a
good place for any of us to live in
unless it is a good place for all
of us to live in.

This, I say, is the real voice of
America. And in this year 1968,
this is the message it will broadcast to America and to the world.

10. STRENGTH AND CHAR-
ACTER OF AMERICANS—
BUSY FACTORIES, FARMS,
CROWDS & TRAFFIC,
ETC.

Let's never forget that despite her
faults, America is a great nation.

11. INTO MONTAGE OF SCE-
NIC VALUES OF AMER-
ICA FROM THE PACIFIC
OCEAN TO DESERTS, TO
SNOW-COVERED MOUN-
TAIN. BESIDE A STILL
POND A MAN WAITS.

R.N.

America is great because her people are great.

With Winston Churchill, we say:
"We have not journeyed all this
way across the centuries, across
the oceans, across the mountains,
across the prairies, because we
are made of sugar candy."

94

VIDEO

12. DOLLY TOWARD SUN-
RISE. HOLD. FADEOUT.

AUDIO

America is in trouble today not
because her people have failed,
but because her leaders have
failed.

What America needs are leaders
to match the greatness of her
people.

MUSIC UP AND OUT.

"Run it through again, would you please, Gene?" Len Garment said. "There's something there that bothers me."

The film was rewound and played again.

"There, that's it," Garment said. "Yeah, that will have to be
changed."

"What will have to be changed?" Jones said.

The film had been stopped just as Richard Nixon, reciting
his litany to the "forgotten Americans," had said, "They provide most of the soldiers who died to keep us free." The picture that went with those words was a close-up of a young
American soldier in Vietnam. A young Negro soldier.

Len Garment was shaking his head.

"We can't show a Negro just as RN's saying 'most of the
soldiers who died to keep us free,'" he said. "That's been one
of their big claims all along—that the draft is unfair to them
—and this could be interpreted in a way that would make us
appear to be taking their side."

"Hey, yes, good point, Len," Frank Shakespeare said.
"That's a very good point."

Harry Treleaven was nodding.

Gene Jones said okay, he would put a white soldier there
instead.

A couple of weeks later, when Treleaven told Gene Jones to shoot a commercial called *Black Capitalism,* he was surprised to hear that Negroes in Harlem were reluctant to pose for the pictures.

Jones had not been able to find any pictures that showed Negroes gainfully employed, so he decided to take his own. He hired his own photographer, a white man, and sent him to Harlem with instructions to take pictures of good Negroes, Negroes who worked and smiled and acted the way white folks thought they ought to. And to take these pictures in front of Negro-owned stores and factories to make the point that this is what honest labor can do for a race.

An hour after he started work, the photographer called Gene Jones and said when he had started lining Negroes up on the street to pose he had been asked by a few young men what he was doing. When he told them he was taking pictures for a Richard Nixon commercial, it was suggested to him that he remove himself and his camera from the vicinity. Fast.

Gene Jones explained to Harry Treleaven.

"Gee, isn't that strange," Treleaven said. "I can't understand an attitude like that."

◄8►

THE FOURTH of the ten scheduled panel shows was done in Philadelphia. It was televised across Pennsylvania and into Delaware and southern New Jersey. Roger Ailes arrived in Philadelphia on Wednesday, September 18, two days before the show was to go on the air.

"We're doing all right," he said. "If we could only get someone to play Hide The Greek." He did not like Spiro Agnew either.

The panel shows, he said, were developing a pattern. "California was bad, because the panel was weak. I'm convinced we need legitimately tough panels to make Nixon give his best. In Ohio, where we just came from, we had a strong panel and it was by far the best show of the three."

The production meeting for the Philadelphia show was held at ten o'clock Thursday morning in the office of Al Hollander, program director of WCAU. The purpose was to acquaint the local staff with what Roger Ailes wanted to do and to acquaint Roger Ailes with the limitations of the local staff. Ailes came in ten minutes late, dressed in sweatshirt and sneakers, coffee cup in hand. He had a room at the Marriott Motor Hotel across the street.

"One problem you're going to have here, Roger," a local man said, "is the size of the studio. You've been working with an audience of three hundred, I understand, but we can only fit two hundred and forty."

"That's all right. I can get as much applause out of two hundred and forty as three hundred, if it's done right, and that's all they are—an applause machine." He paused. "That and a couple of reaction shots.

"I'm more concerned," Ailes said, "about where camera one is. I've talked to Nixon twice about playing to it and I can't seem to get through to him. So I think this time we're going to play it to him."

"You ought to talk to him about saying, 'Let me make one thing very clear' ten times every show," someone said. "It's driving people nuts."

"I have, and Shakespeare told me not to mention it again. It bugs Nixon. Apparently everybody has been telling him about it but he can't stop."

After half an hour, Roger Ailes left the meeting. "Fuck it," he said. "Those things bore me. I'll leave Rourke to walk around and kick the tires." He went across the street to the motel. The morning was clear and hot.

"The problem with the panels is that we need variety," Ailes said. "Nixon gets bored with the same kind of people. We've got to screw around with this one a little bit."

"You still want seven?" an assistant, supplied by the local Republicans, asked.

"Yes. And on this one we definitely need a Negro. I don't think it's necessary to have one in every group of six people, no matter what our ethnic experts say, but in Philadelphia it is. *U.S. News and World Report* this week says that one of every three votes cast in Philadelphia will be Negro. And goddammit, we're locked into the thing, anyway. Once you start it's hard as hell to stop, because the press will pick it up and make a big deal out of why no Negro all of a sudden."

"I know one in Philadelphia," the local man, whose name was Dan Buser, said. "He's a dynamic type, the head of a self-help organization, that kind of thing. And he is black."

"What do you mean, he's black?"

"I mean he's dark. It will be obvious on television that he's not white."

"You mean we won't have to put a sign around him that says, 'This is our Negro'?"

"Absolutely not."

"Fine. Call him. Let's get this thing going."

"Nixon is better if the panel is offbeat," Ailes was saying. "It's tough to get an articulate ditchdigger, but I'd like to."

"I have one name here," Buser said. "Might be offbeat. A Pennsylvania Dutch farmer."

"No! No more farmers. They all ask the same goddamn dull questions."

The morning produced an Italian lawyer from Pittsburgh, a liberal housewife from the Main Line, and a Young Republican from the Wharton School of Business.

"Now we need a newsman," Roger Ailes said.

I suggested the name of an articulate political reporter from the *Evening Bulletin* in Philadelphia.

"Fine. Why don't you call him?"

"He's a Negro."

"Oh, shit, we can't have two. Even in Philadelphia. Wait a minute—call him, and if he'll do it we can drop the self-help guy."

But the reporter was unavailable. Then I suggested Jack McKinney, a radio talk-show host from WCAU. Ailes called him and after half an hour on the phone, McKinney, who found it hard to believe the show would not be rigged, agreed to go on.

Then I suggested a psychiatrist I knew: the head of a group that brought Vietnamese children wounded in the war to the United States for treatment and artificial limbs.

"What's his name?"

"Herb Needleman."

Roger Ailes called him. Herb Needleman agreed to do the show. Roger Ailes was pleased. "The guy sounded tough but not hysterical. This is shaping up as a very interesting show."

A newsman from Camden, New Jersey, was added, and, at four o'clock, Ailes called Len Garment in New York to tell him the panel was complete.

". . . that's six," he was saying, "and then we've got a Jewish doctor from Philadelphia, a psychiatrist, who— Wait a minute, Len, relax. . . . I—yes, he's already accepted, the . . . Well, why not? . . . Are you serious? . . . Honest to God, Len? . . . Oh, no, I can get out of it, it'll just be a little embarrassing . . . No, you're right, if he feels that strongly about it. . . ."

Roger Ailes hung up.

"Jesus Christ," he said. "You're not going to believe this but Nixon hates psychiatrists."

"What?"

"Nixon hates psychiatrists. He's got this thing, apparently. They make him very nervous. You should have heard Len on the phone when I told him I had one on the panel. Did you hear him? If I've ever heard a guy's voice turn white, that was it."

"Why?"

"He said he didn't want to go into it. But apparently Nixon won't even let one in the same room. Jesus Christ, could you picture him on a live TV show finding out he's being questioned by a shrink?"

There was another reason, too, why Herb Needleman was unacceptable. "Len says they want to go easy on Jews for a while. I guess Nixon's tired of saying 'balance of power' about the goddamn Middle East."

So, at 4:15 P.M., Roger Ailes made another call to Dr. Needleman, to tell him that this terribly embarrassing thing had happened, that the show had been overbooked. Something about having to add a panelist from New Jersey because the show would be televised into the southern part of the state.

"You know what I'd like?" Ailes said later. "As long as we've got this extra spot open. A good, mean, Wallaceite cab driver. Wouldn't that be great? Some guy to sit there and say, 'Awright, mac, what about these niggers?' "

It was five o'clock in the afternoon. The day still was hot but Roger Ailes had not been outside since morning. Air conditioning, iced tea and the telephone.

"Lyn," he said to his secretary, "call room service and order me a steak. Anybody else want anything? Yes, order us all a steak. And tell them to hurry up. It took forty-five minutes to get coffee and danish this morning."

Forty-five minutes later, nothing had arrived.

"Find out what's holding up that order. No, wait a minute. Never mind. Tell them to forget it. We'll go out to eat."

"They say it's already left, Roger. It's on its way."

"Tell them if it isn't here, in this room, in three minutes, I'm sending it back."

Five minutes later nothing had arrived. "Come on," Roger Ailes said. "Let's go find a cab driver."

"What about the dinners?" his secretary asked.

"Send them back."

"I can't do that."

"Send them back, goddammit!"

He stepped out to the motel parking lot and walked through the sun to the main entrance. The Marriott was the best place they had in Philadelphia. Eight cabs were lined up in the driveway. The third driver Roger Ailes talked to said he was not really for Wallace, but he wasn't against him either.

"What's your name?" Roger Ailes said.

"Frank Kornsey."

"You want to go on television tomorrow night?—right across the street there—and ask Mr. Nixon some questions. Any questions you want."

"I've got to work tomorrow night."

"Take it off. Tell them why. We'll pay you for the hours you miss, plus your expenses to and from the studio."

"My wife will think I'm nuts."

"Your wife will love you. When did she ever think she'd be married to a guy who conversed with the next President of the United States?"

"I'll let you know in the morning," Frank Kornsey said.

The food had come to the motel room and the secretary had not sent it back. Roger Ailes was unhappy about this but he ate. The talk drifted to some of the curious associations into which Nixon seemed to fall. People he sought to align himself with, whose endorsement he was so pleased to accept, when even in political terms they probably did him more harm than good. He was trying to escape his 1950s image (while promising a restoration of the period) yet he encouraged ties to celebrities who were already stale by the time of his first campaign. John Wayne, Bud Wilkinson, Connie Francis.

"That's where he's ill advised," Roger Ailes said. "He

doesn't know his ass from his elbow about who's who and neither do those guys around him."

"That Wilkinson, for Christ's sake, he's like a marionette with the strings broken," Ailes's director said. The director had come over from the studio in midafternoon, after working on final placement of the cameras.

"Oh, Wilkinson's a sweet guy," Ailes said, "but he's got absolutely no sense of humor."

"If you're going to keep using him as moderator, you should tell him to stop applauding all the answers."

"He's been told," Ailes said, "he's been told. He just can't help it."

Ailes got up from the table. "Let's face it, a lot of people think Nixon is dull. Think he's a bore, a pain in the ass. They look at him as the kind of kid who always carried a bookbag. Who was forty-two years old the day he was born. They figure other kids got footballs for Christmas, Nixon got a briefcase and he loved it. He'd always have his homework done and he'd never let you copy.

"Now you put him on television, you've got a problem right away. He's a funny-looking guy. He looks like somebody hung him in a closet overnight and he jumps out in the morning with his suit all bunched up and starts running around saying, 'I want to be President.' I mean this is how he strikes some people. That's why these shows are important. To make them forget all that."

Richard Nixon came to Philadelphia the next day: Friday. There was the standard downtown motorcade at noon. Frank Kornsey took the whole day off to stay home and write questions. "I got some beauties," he told Roger Ailes on the phone.

Ailes went to the studio at two o'clock in the afternoon. "I'm going to fire this fucking director," he said. "I'm going to fire the son of a bitch right after the show. Look at this. Look at the positioning of these cameras. I've told him fifty times I want close-ups. Close-ups! This is a close-up medium. It's dull to shoot chest shots. I want to see faces. I want to see pores. That's what people are. That's what television is."

He walked through the studio, shaking his head. "We won't get a shot better than waist high from these cameras all night. That's nineteen forty-eight direction. When you had four people in every shot and figured you were lucky you had any shot at all."

The director explained his technical problems.

"I don't give a fuck about the seats. I'll give up thirty seats to get a tight shot."

The director explained some more.

"I don't care! I don't want to hear that shit! I told you what I wanted and it's your job to give it to me. Not to set things up your own way and then have me walk in and find it like this four hours before the show. I want close-ups, and I don't want to hear about the limitations of the zoom lenses or any other goddamn things. It can be done. I've done it myself when I've directed and I want it done tonight."

The audience filled the studio at seven o'clock. The panel was brought in at 7:15. Frank Kornsey was nervous. Roger Ailes offered him a shot of bourbon. "No, thanks," he said. "I'll be all right." He tried to grin.

At 7:22 Jack Rourke stepped onto the riser. He was a heavy Irishman with a red face and gray hair. "Hello," he said to the audience. "I'm Frank Sinatra."

The Nixon family, David Eisenhower, and the governor of

Pennsylvania came in. The audience applauded. This audience, like the others, had been carefully recruited by the local Republican organization. "That's the glee club," Jack Rourke said, pointing to the Nixons.

The director walked into the control booth at 7:24. "He's crazy," the director said, meaning Roger Ailes. "He has no conception of the mechanical limitations involved in a show like this. He says he wants close-ups, it's like saying he wants to go to the moon."

The director took his seat at the control panel and spoke to a cameraman on the floor. "Make sure you know where Mrs. Nixon is and what she looks like."

A member of the Nixon staff ran into the booth. "Cut the sound in that studio next door. We've got the press in there and we don't want them to hear the warmup."

"Now, when Mr. Nixon comes in," Jack Rourke was saying, "I want you to tear the place apart. Sound like ten thousand people. I'm sure, of course, that you'll also want to stand up at that point. So what do you say we try it now. Come on, stand up. And let me hear it."

"One forty-five to air," the director said in the control booth.

"Tell Rourke to check the sound level on the panel."

Jack Rourke turned to Frank Kornsey. "Ask a question, please. We'd like to check your microphone."

Frank Kornsey leaned forward and spoke, barely above a whisper. His list of "beauties" lay on a desk before him. He was still pale, even through his makeup.

"I was just wondering how Mr. and Mrs. Nixon are enjoying our wonderful city of Philadelphia," he said.

Pat Nixon, in a first-row seat, gave her tight, closemouthed smile.

"No, they don't care for it," Jack Rourke said.

"Thirty seconds," came a voice from the control room. "Clear the decks, please, thirty seconds."

Then, at exactly 7:30, while a tape of Richard Nixon's motorcade was being played for the viewers at home, the director said, "Okay, cue the applause, move back camera one, move back one," and Richard Nixon stepped through a crack in a curtain, hunched his shoulders, raised his arms, wiggled his wrists, made V-signs with his fingers, and switched on his grin.

Jack McKinney, the talk-show host, was wearing his hairpiece for the occasion. Nixon turned to him first, still with the grin, hands clasped before him, into his fourth show now and over the jitters. Maybe, in fact, ready to show off just a bit. A few new combinations, if the proper moment came, to please the crowd.

"Yes, Mr. McKinney," he said.

Jack McKinney did not lead with his right but he threw a much stiffer jab than Nixon had been expecting: Why are you so reluctant to comment on Vietnam this year when in 1952, faced with a similar issue in Korea, you were so free with your partisan remarks?

Not a crippling question, but there was an undertone of unfriendliness to it. Worse, it had been put to him in professional form. Nixon had been expecting, maybe, a request for comment on the war, to which he would have given the standard With-Peace-Negotiations-At-Such-A-Delicate-Stage reply. But here was a question which assumed that reply and requested that it be defended, in light of a seeming contradiction. Nixon stepped back, a bit off balance. This sort of thing threatened the stability of the whole format; the basis being the hypothesis that Nixon could appear to risk all by going live while in fact risking nothing by facing the loose syntax and predictable, sloppy thrusts of amateurs.

Nixon threw up an evasive flurry. But the grin was gone from his face. Not only did he know now that he would have to be careful of McKinney, he was forced to wonder, for the first time, what he might encounter from the others.

The Negro was next, which was poor placement, but god-dammit, he couldn't just skip right past the man, searching for a patsy while he rested. He would have to proceed nor-mally and hope that predictability would return.

Warily: "Yes, Mr. Burress." And Burress laid Black Capi-talism right down the middle, straight and soft. Nixon had it memorized. He took a long time on the answer, though, sa-voring its clichés, making sure his wind had come back all the way.

Then Frank Kornsey, who studied his list and asked: "What are you going to do about the Pueblo?" Beautiful. Nixon had been honing this one to perfection. He had taken 1:22 with it in California, according to Roger Ailes's chart, but had brought it down to 1:05 in Ohio. Now he delivered it in less than a minute. He was smooth again, and grinning, as he turned to the liberal housewife, Mrs. Mather.

Was civil disobedience *ever* justified, she wondered. Nixon took a quick step backwards on the riser. His face fell into the solemnity mask. There were philosophic implications there he did not like. He could understand the impatience of those less fortunate than ourselves, he assured her, and their demand for immediate improvement was, indeed, healthy for our society in many ways. But, as long as change could be brought about within the system—and no, he was not like some who claimed it could not—then there was no cause, repeat, *no* cause that justified the breaking of a law.

But he knew he would have to watch her, too. The first line of sweat broke out across his upper lip.

The Young Republican from Wharton wanted to know

how to bring the McCarthy supporters back into the mainstream, which was fine, but then the newsman from Camden asked if Nixon agreed with Spiro Agnew's charge that Hubert Humphrey was "soft on communism."

He knew how to handle that one, but while sidestepping he noted that this fellow, too, semed unawed. That made three out of seven who were ready, it appeared, to mix it up. And one of them a good-looking articulate woman. And another, McKinney, who seemed truly mean.

It was McKinney's turn again: Why was Nixon refusing to appear on any of the news confrontation shows such as Meet the Press? Why would he face the public only in staged settings such as this, where the questions were almost certain to be worded generally enough to allow him any vague sort of answer he wanted to give? Where the presence of the cheering studio audience was sure to intimidate any questioner who contemplated true engagement? Where Nixon moved so quickly from one questioner to the next that he eliminated any possibility of follow-up, any chance for true discussion . . . ?

"The guy's making a speech!" Frank Shakespeare shouted in the control booth. Roger Ailes jumped for the phone to Wilkinson on stage. But McKinney was finished, for the moment. The question was, had he finished Nixon, too?

"I've done those quiz shows, Mr. McKinney. I've done them until they were running out of my ears." There was no question on one point: Richard Nixon was upset.

Staring hard at McKinney, he grumbled something about why there should be more fuss about Hubert Humphrey not having press conferences and less about him and Meet the Press.

It did not seem much of a recovery but in the control room Frank Shakespeare punched the palm of one hand with the fist of the other and said, "That socks it to him, Dickie Baby!" The audience cheered. Suddenly, Nixon, perhaps sensing a weakness in McKinney where he had feared that none existed, perhaps realizing he had no choice, surely buoyed by the cheers, decided to slug it out.

"Go ahead," he said, gesturing. "I want you to follow up."

McKinney came back creditably, using the word "amorphous" and complaining that viewers were being asked to support Nixon for President on the basis of "nothing but a wink and a smile" particularly in regard to Vietnam.

"Now, Mr. McKinney, maybe I haven't been as specific . . . ," and Nixon was off on a thorough rephrasing of his Vietnam nonposition, which, while it contained no substance—hence, could not accommodate anything new— sounded, to uninitiates, like a public step forward. The audience was ecstatic. Outnumbered, two hundred forty-one to one, McKinney could do nothing but smile and shake his head.

"Be very careful with McKinney," Shakespeare said, bending over Roger Ailes. "I want to give him a chance but I don't want him to hog the show."

"Yeah, if he starts making another speech I'll call Bud and—"

But Shakespeare no longer was listening. He was grappling with a cameraman who had come into the control booth and begun to take pictures of the production staff at work.

"No press," Shakespeare said, and when the man continued shooting his film, Shakespeare began to push. The cameraman pushed back as well as he could, but Shakespeare, leaning hard, edged him toward the door.

"I was given permission—"

"No one is given permission—"

"Now wait a minute—"

"Wait nothing, we'll talk outside—"

And Frank Shakespeare pushed the cameraman through the doorway and into a hall outside.

Meanwhile, Frank Kornsey, consulting his written list again, had asked: "What do you intend to do about the gun control law?" Then, quickly, the others: Are you writing off the black vote? What about federal tax credits . . . water and air pollution . . . and then the Camden newsman, whose name was Flynn, asking about Nixon's action in 1965 when he had called for the removal of a Rutgers history professor who had spoken kindly of the Viet Cong—on campus.

Nixon assured Mr. Flynn that academic freedom remained high on his personal list of privileges which all Americans should enjoy, but added, "There is one place where I would draw the line.

"And that is, I do not believe that anyone who is paid by the government and who is using government facilities—and Rutgers, as I'm sure you are aware, Mr. Flynn, is a state institution—has the right to call for the victory of the enemy over American boys—while he is on the campus."

But now McKinney gathered himself for a final try. "You said that the Rutgers professor 'called for' the victory of the Viet Cong, but as I recall he didn't say that at all. This is what I mean about your being able, on this kind of show, to slide off the questions. Now, the facts were—"

"Oh, I know the facts, Mr. McKinney. I know the facts."

Nixon was grinning. The audience poured forth its loudest applause of the night. Bud Wilkinson joined in, full of righteous fervor. Of course Mr. Nixon knew the facts.

McKinney was beaten but he would not quit.

"The facts were that the professor did not 'call for' the victory—"

"No, what he said, Mr. McKinney, and I believe I am quoting him *exactly*, was that he would 'welcome the impending victory of the Viet Cong.'"

"Which is not the same thing."

"Well, Mr. McKinney, you can make that distinction if you wish, but what I'll do is I'll turn it over to the television audience right now and let them decide for themselves about the semantics. About the difference between 'calling for' and 'welcoming' a victory of the Viet Cong."

He was angry but he had it under control and he talked fast and hard and when he was finished he swung immediately to the next questioner. The show was almost over. McKinney was through for the night.

"Boy, is he going to be pissed," Roger Ailes said as he hurried down from the control room. "He'll think we really tried to screw him. But critically it was the best show he's done."

Roger Ailes went looking for Nixon. He wound up in an elevator with Nixon's wife. She was wearing a green dress and she did not smile. One thought of the remark a member of the Nixon staff had made: "Next to her, RN looks like Mary Poppins."

"Hello, Mrs. Nixon," Roger Ailes said.

She nodded. She had known him for months.

"How did you like the show?" he asked.

She nodded very slowly; her mouth was drawn in a thin, straight line.

"Everyone seems to think it was by far the best," Ailes said. "Especially the way he took care of that McKinney."

Pat Nixon stared at the elevator door. The car stopped. The door opened. She got off and moved down a hallway with the secret service men around her.

◄9►

Gene Jones made eighteen commercials for Richard Nixon. All were done with still pictures except for E.S.J. #16: *Woman,* which was done directly on movie film. This one was designed to scare people. It showed a woman walking down a lonely city street late at night, Eighty-fifth Street at Columbus Avenue in New York City to be exact. Jones had the police close it off so he could film. There was an announcer—not Nixon, this time—telling how a violent crime was committed in America every sixty seconds. Watching it, you were sure the woman would not make it to the end of the street, or the end of the commercial, without being mugged. But she did.

Gene Jones had trouble finding an actress to play the part of the woman. He talked to four one morning and when they heard it was for Richard Nixon they all said no. Jones could not understand this. Negroes, yes; he could see why Negroes were hostile. But actresses he could not figure out.

And then when he finally found one, he had to shoot the film sixteen times before he was satisfied that he had got the right look of "controlled anxiety" on the woman's face.

When all the commercials were finally made, Jim Sage, who was Gene Jones's top assistant, put them together on a single reel. Sage had a feeling that there was something important happening here. That this was not just politics and not just advertising and not just using television in a campaign, but something new and undefined.

Sage was a McCarthy Democrat who was doing the Nixon work because Gene Jones wanted him to and he thought enough of Gene Jones not to say no. But Sage was suffering. Eighteen straight had been too much. He was blinded by rosy sunsets, choking on the smoke from America's bustling factories, and sick to death of towheaded little kids romping in the sun.

But he could not get rid of the idea that somehow this was history. Finally, he called a couple of men he knew at the Museum of Modern Art. He suggested that all the pictures taken together, with an explanation of how they had been used in each commercial, would make a strong exhibit. The museum men agreed to come and at least look at the reel which contained the eighteen spots.

Before he showed the film, Sage explained a little of the background.

"The script," he told them, "in most cases is very, very basic. We try to create an atmosphere through our selection of pictures. We have one thousand stills in the office right now. We pay between one hundred and fifty and two hundred and fifty dollars for the rights to use each picture once. That's not for the picture—just for the right to use it once. The total cost of each commercial will probably wind up somewhere around twenty-five thousand.

"The use of stills for propaganda purposes—or 'persuasion,' as they like to say—is still quite new. There could be a use for the technique even beyond the campaign. Maybe the State of the Union address, for instance, will be intercut with still photographs.

"The problem we've had, in most cases, is Nixon himself.

He says such incredible pap. In fact, the radicalness of this approach is in the fact of creating an image without actually saying anything. The words are given meaning by the impressions created by the stills."

The museum men made no comment until the reel was done. Until all of the steel girders, sunsets, mountain peaks and bare-assed little kids had passed.

Then the first museum man spoke: "I'll say one thing. It's easy to tell the good guys from the bad guys."

"What do you mean?"

"The good guys are either children, soldiers or over fifty years old."

The second museum man was shaking his head.

"I don't believe it," he said. "This is incredible. Every god-damned cliché in the book. There's not one—not one—that you've missed."

"Insidious, isn't it?" Jim Sage said.

"No, it's not insidious," the museum man said. "It's just trite." Then they picked up their umbrellas and they left.

"Asses," Jim Sage said. "They missed the whole point." The rain was pouring down outside. The morning was dark and cold. The point was that the commercials were supposed to be trite. They had to be to move the audience they would reach. Their message was intended for people who had trite-ness oozing out of every pore. Persons who, as in Harry Treleaven's description of Spiro Agnew, had never made an original observation in their lives. Gene Jones had not expected that the head of the motion picture department of the New York Museum of Modern Art would be impressed with colored photographs of steel girders being swung into place.

"You know," Sage said, "what we're really seeing here is a

genesis. We're moving into a period where a man is going to be merchandised on television more and more. It upsets you and me, maybe, but we're not typical Americans. The public sits home and watches *Gunsmoke* and when they're fed this pap about Nixon they think they're getting something worth-while."

Sage was the only member of the staff who really enjoyed talking about the theory of the sixty-second spot. Jones had said only that spots "are supposed to get the audience's attention in a very obtrusive way. Knock them down. Not give them a chance." But Sage liked to analyze.

"Remember," he said, as the rain poured down, "that man's voice you just heard over and over again inside might wind up as President in a very few weeks."

"Probably will."

"Probably will. The most powerful man in the world. And he's going to be elected on what he didn't say. He's created an image of himself through cornball sunsets and WASP-y faces and no one remembers what he says. Which is gobbledy-gook anyway, of course. But they do remember 'Love' on the helmet. Those images stick.

"We didn't have to make cheap and vulgar films, you know. We're capable of doing more. All of us are, as individuals and as a team. But those images strike a note of recognition in the kind of people to whom we are trying to appeal. The kind of person who might vote for Nixon in the first place.

"Nixon has not only developed the use of the platitude, he's raised it to an art form. It's mashed potatoes. It appeals to the lowest common denominator of American taste. It's a farce, a delicious farce; self-deception carried to the nth degree.

"We are made of sugar candy after all. We insulate ourselves by these visions from the reality of Vietnam, from the reality of children starving in Biafra. The commercials are successful because people are able to relate them to their own delightful misconceptions of themselves and their country.

"Have you noticed? The same faces reappear in different spots. The same pictures are used again and again. They become symbols, recurring like notes in an orchestrated piece. The Alabama sharecropper with the vacant stare, the vigorous young steelworker, the grinning soldier . . .

"And the rosier the sunset, the more wholesome the smiling face, the more it conforms to their false vision of what they are and what their country is."

"So it really is insidious?"

"Oh, I don't know. The effect is, but I don't know that we are in our intent. If we were really being charlatans we would give much more study to the psychological part—the overall effect of the relationship of one still to another. But these people aren't that smart. They're fools, in fact. Even in their choice of pictures they betray uncertainty about what they're really after. That's because they don't *know* what they're after. Their product is amorphous—it has to be amorphous—because so are they. I don't mean Gene now, I mean the Nixon people. All running around here with their identical expressions and their identical dark suits. The three blind mice.

"And no matter how trite our product was, it wasn't trite enough for them. They had to change something in every single spot. The riot commercial originally ended with a picture of a Negro boy staring into the smoldering ruins of what had been his home. That had to go: for political reasons, they said. They were afraid they'd be accused of trying to stir up sympathy for Negroes who riot. We also had to drop a shot of a group of Negroes looking at the same kind of thing. It wasn't bland enough. We had to use uninhabited ruins.

"In the Democratic convention spot we had to cut shots of Daley calling Ribicoff whatever it was that he called him, because their surveys had shown most Americans approved of the way Daley acted. So we shoved in more bland faces. In the Youth commercial we had hippies who looked like they enjoyed it. That had to come out. We could not give the impression that there was happiness to be found outside the mainstream.

"The goddamned idiots. I remember one afternoon they were all over here looking at one of the pieces and it just wasn't right; there was just something missing. They were all standing around wondering what was wrong and Shakespeare turned to me and said, 'What do you think is the problem here?' And I told him. 'Well, for one thing you don't have a single shot of a Negro—not one black face.'

"And he turned to me with this incredulous sort of look in his eye and said: 'But we've got an Indian.'"

Jim Sage smiled. "To get back to being insidious, yes: the effect of the stills can be almost subliminal. In less than a minute you can get up to forty images, each with a different time, place and face, so you can create an impression that is altogether different from what is being said. If, for instance, you were to turn off Nixon's voice and play a Bach fugue or Vivaldi, you could read anything you wanted into it."

One night, toward the end of the campaign, as he sat in his office, Gene Jones said, "Look, I get it from my friends, too, I go to a party and the first thing everybody wants to know is, how can you work for that fascist bastard."

He shrugged.

"I'm a professional. This is a professional job. I was neutral toward Nixon when I started. Now I happen to be for him.

But that's not the point. The point is, for the money, I'd do it for almost anybody.

"My one qualm about Nixon," Gene Jones said, "is that I'm not sure he's got the sensitivity he should. To Appalachia, to the slums, to the poverty and destitution that reside there. I don't know whether as a human being he's actually got that sensitivity.

"I hope he has, because it's really awful, when you think of all the things wrong inside this country now. The hatred, the violence, the cities gone to hell. And the war. All our kids getting killed in that goddamned war."

He stood, ready to go upstairs, to the third-floor production room, to touch up one of the final spots.

"What are you going to do when this is all over?" I said.

"Move out."

"Yes, I know you're leaving this studio, but I mean where are you going to work next, what are you going to do?"

"No, I didn't mean move out of the studio," he said. "I mean move out of the country. I'm not going to live here anymore."

"What?"

"I've bought myself some land in the Caribbean—on the island of Montsarrat—and that's where I'm going as soon as this is over."

"Permanently?"

"Yes, permanently," he said. And then he talked about the direct plane service from Montsarrat to New York, Toronto, and London, and about how America was no place to bring up kids anymore. And all this against the background of the commercials he had made: with the laughing, playing children and the green grass and the sunsets and Richard Nixon saying over and over again what wonderful people we all were and what a wonderful place we lived in.

". . . I really don't see any choice," Gene Jones said. "I mean, I don't want my kids growing up in an atmosphere like this."

Then he excused himself and went upstairs.

◄10►

FRED LARUE was getting bald and he smoked cigars. He was from Atlanta, Georgia. His job was to persuade people in the South not to vote for George Wallace, but he had to do it in a way that would not upset people in the rest of the country.

In early October, it did not look as if he had done this job very well. South of Baltimore, Wallace seemed immense.

In fact, on the morning of the day I saw Fred LaRue, I said to Harry Treleaven, "I'm going up to headquarters this afternoon to learn about the southern strategy." And Treleaven laughed and said, "If you find out what it is, please tell me."

Fred LaRue did not talk very colorfully but he wrote memos. There was one he wrote on September 7 in which he summed up what he was gonig to do in the South.

"The anti-Wallace message will be indirect—'between the lines' and in 'regional code words,'" he wrote. He, like the rest of them, was afraid of being obvious. It was all right to chase the Wallace vote but not all right to get caught.

"One example of the propaganda innovations to be employed," LaRue wrote, "is a special ballad-type song in the current 'country and western' music style, by which nationally famous artists will 'sing' the message via the radio and TV. The multi-stanza ballad will allow issues to be included or excluded as the local situation indicates. The song's technical aspects will be such that 'local talent' as well as a variety of 'stars' can render it effectively. . . ."

The name of the song was "Bring Our Country Back":

> *How far down the road has our country gone,*
> *In this time of trouble and strife?*
> *How can we bring our country back*
> *To the good and decent life?*
>
> *Have we gone so far that we can't return?*
> *Have we lost our place in the sun?*
> *Yes, we can bring our country back,*
> *But it's up to everyone!*
>
> *This time, this time, your precious vote*
> *   will get the big job done*
> *This time, this time, your vote can bring*
> *   a change in Washington.*

(Alternate verses and chorus changes)

> *Tell me where's there a man . . . in this fair land*
> *Who can get us back on the track?*
> *Dick Nixon is a decent man*
> *Who can bring our country back.*
>
> *Our votes can bring our country back*
> *But it's up to everyone!*
>
> *This time, this time, with leadership*
> *   from Richard M. Nixon.*

"But let me tell you something," Fred LaRue said. "You could spend a million dollars on songs like that and it's wasted money unless you get them played in the right spots. You got to get that on or adjacent to country and western programs. Either that or wrestling. That's a special kind of audience. The people that watch country and western and wrestling. What you do for those people would not appeal to other kinds of people and vice versa. Now you take Orlando, Florida, for instance. There is no country and western show in town there, so we go to wrestling instead."

Then Fred LaRue went into his desk and pulled out a list of the radio programs on which "Bring Our Country Back" was being played. There were the singing shows of such people as Bill Anderson, Buck Owens, Ernest Tubb, and the Wilburn Brothers, and such specials as the Wally Fowler Gospel Hour and Chattahoochee RFD.

The problem was in finding country and western singers to do the song. Most were backing Wallace. Finally Fred LaRue went back to the 1940s and '50s and found Roy Acuff and Tex Ritter and Stuart Hamblen.

Then he explained about the other southern commercials. These had been provided by the Thurmond Speaks Committee of South Carolina. A lot of them had Thurmond himself talking about crime and bussing and the Supreme Court. They were used, LaRue said, "very selectively," which meant they would never be heard in New York.

LaRue, in fact, had a map of the South on the wall of his office. Little green and red and yellow pins were stuck all through it. The red and yellow pins represented areas in which the Thurmond commercials were being used, while the green pins represented those locations to which Senator Thurmond had personally carried the campaign.

All this was advertising which Harry Treleaven had noth-

ing to do with. He did not even see it. He was considered
Madison Avenue, and it was felt that Madison Avenue did
not understand the South.

Kevin Phillips, the "ethnic specialist," was twenty-seven
years old, pale and dour. He worked at a desk in a hallway
because by the time he had been hired all the offices at headquarters had been filled.

"It took awhile to get programed," he said, "but I've been
effectively plugged in since late August."

This was how he always talked. Len Garment called him
"The Computer." Roger Ailes swore he was stuffed with saw-
dust.

"Essentially what I do is determine what blocs can be
moved in what states by what approach," he said. " 'Group
susceptibility' I call it.

"For instance, in Wisconsin you have Germans and you
have Scandinavians, and the two groups respond to very
different things. First, we determine where the groups are
and then we decide how to reach them. What radio station
each listens to, and so forth. I started too late to do it properly this year, but by 'seventy-two I should have it broken
down county by county across the whole country so we'll be
able to zero in on a much more refined target."

Kevin Phillips had graduated from Colgate and the Har-
vard Law School and had been administrative assistant to
Paul Fino, a congressman from New York City. Besides
working for Nixon, he was writing a book about American
voting patterns which the Conservative Book Club was going to publish.

He was convinced that a Conservative revolution was
sweeping America. He kept saying things like, "The Demo-

cratic party will not carry Oklahoma again for the rest of this century." Then he would go into a desk drawer and pull out the results of surveys made among sixth-graders in St. Louis and the Bronx which proved that they were far more conservative than their parents.

"It's happening," he would say. "It is really coming to pass. But no one sees it. No one knows."

He said he was very highly respected at headquarters. When he had first come to work, there had been a real computer doing his job. Some people from MIT were running it. He disposed of them immediately.

"The first time I checked their stuff I took them apart so badly that I never saw them or heard from them again. Now, I'm plugged in absolutely. Any memorandum I write gets to the top of the heap in five minutes."

One of his big jobs was to help Fred LaRue with the South. "When a northerner designs anti-Wallace stuff, it's bad stuff," he said. "It's tricky, smoothie, smacks of the Establishment. This doesn't work. You don't mock this guy. You don't talk about his wife being a clerk in a five-and-ten-cent store. A lot of people are clerks in five-and-ten-cent stores and they have cousins all over Alabama."

Phillips would take the reports of people like John Maddox, the Semantic Differential man, and analyze them and make specific strategy suggestions.

For instance, Maddox recently had written, "Billy Graham is the second most revered man in the South among adult voters." It was not made clear whether Wallace or Christ ranked first, but the message was plain: Be pals with Billy Graham and publicize the friendship.

The same Maddox report said, "the simple folksy manner of John Wayne can be effective with the target group." And that, Kevin Phillips said, was an insight.

"Wayne might sound bad to people in New York, but he sounds great to the schmucks we're trying to reach through John Wayne. The people down there along the Yahoo Belt. If I had the time I'd check to see in what areas *The Green Berets* was held over and I'd play a special series of John Wayne spots wherever it was."

Another thing Kevin Phillips did was evaluate the Gene Jones commercials and make recommendations as to how they should be used.

He wrote things like: "*Great Nation:* This is fine for national use, but viz local emphasis it strikes me as best suited to the South and heartland. They will like the great nation self-help, fields of waving wheat stuff and the general thrust of Protestant ethic imagery."

And: "*Order:* Entirely suitable for national use, emphasis on cities which have had riots (Cal., Ill., Ohio, Mich., Pa., N.J.) . . . and in the South to reinforce RN's hard-line image."

Beyond this, Phillips made suggestions for future Gene Jones spots.

"We need a red-hot military music, land of pride and glory special for the South and Border. I think that this is very important. Secondarily, we need a more concern for the countryside, its values and farmers welfare spot, complete with threshing threshers, siloes, Aberdeen Angus herds, et al.

"Look," he said, "I have no interest in how many voters can fit on the head of a pin. All I care about is how many we can get out there by hook or by crook who will vote for us."

◄11►

In October, everyone suddenly got scared. Two weeks earlier, Harry Treleaven had flown to Key Biscayne for a weekend strategy meeting and had returned saying that Nixon's election was assured. He said they had even decided to cut the budget in certain states such as California and Illinois, where Nixon was so far ahead it seemed silly to spend the money.

But now the bubble had burst. The months of staleness were catching up.

Nixon's lead in the polls was getting smaller. The official word was not to worry, not to make any changes, but behind it there was uneasiness. John Mitchell could say as many times as he wanted that it was only normal, that it had to happen after they had been so far ahead for so long, but that did not change the figures. Nor did it change the sense of helplessness and the first faint traces of fear that were starting to creep up from deep inside. It was like when the stock market begins to fall and everyone has reasons but no one really *knows,* and no one knows either how far down it will go.

Because they were so satisfied with themselves—and why shouldn't they have been, after what they had accomplished in nine months—they looked outside for reasons. Rumors of the bomb halt, they said: that was a big part of the trouble. Maybe they were right.

But there was more. There was the cumulative effect of almost three hundred days of Richard Nixon imposed upon a nation in a year of fighting and killing and hate. Almost three hundred days of the grin. Of the wiggling, pointing fingers. Of the resonant, hollow voice.

Almost three hundred days in which Americans who were not bankers or corporation vice presidents or insurance salesmen or lawyers who defended only clients who could pay became aware of the truth that Gloria Steinem, the writer, would put into a phrase in December: We're all niggers now.

The image campaign had done all it could within its limits. But its limits were the man. Richard Nixon. Who had as his best friend a man named Bebe Rebozo, who dealt in real estate in southern Florida. Whose daughter would be married in a ceremony performed by Norman Vincent Peale. To a grandson of Eisenhower. Richard Nixon, whose authorized biography, a part of the literature of the campaign, said: "Nixon belongs to impressive in-town clubs—Metropolitan, Links, Recess—and fashionable country clubs—Blind Brook in Westchester, Baltusrol in New Jersey."

We had seen the mules in the hot Atlanta street and heard the sobs of children inside the crowded church as they buried Martin Luther King. And watched Bob Kennedy's life spill across the gray hotel kitchen floor, and taken the train ride and seen black men cry again, and we had cried with them. And now this Nixon came out of his country clubs which he had worked so hard to make and he waved his credit cards in our face.

It had always been there—this feeling that allowed Harry Treleaven to wonder why his white photographer was not received in Harlem with grace—but it had been obscured.

By the memo writers: Buchanan, Price, and Gavin; and by Treleaven, Shakespeare, Garment, and Roger Ailes. Obscured also by what Gene McCarthy did, and by Chicago, and the hatred which consumed that city and grew out of what was left.

All this obscured Richard Nixon, who did not want America playing on his lawn. And then, in a moment when Hubert Humphrey paused for breath, America—that portion of it which Nixon wanted so badly to forget—began to come alive.

He would not debate. He would not go on the question shows. He said sock it to 'em everywhere he went and balloons were sent into the sky in a restrained and organized way. He wanted no part of the campus. The city slum was a foreign country, and this was one whose leaders did not receive him with backslaps and hugs.

People were saying that the President of the United States might soon stop dropping bombs that killed people no American had ever seen. The men who worked for Richard Nixon were infuriated by the rumor. That bastard, they said. He's going to stop dropping bombs.

All the while, Richard Nixon, in his stiff, mechanical way, did the things he thought a presidential candidate trying to hold a lead should do. A burnt-out case; hanging on.

"Everybody has the jitters," Harry Treleaven said. "They all feel a change. They haven't a single damn figure to prove it but they can feel the undecided vote going to Humphrey."

Nixon went to Boston for the New England panel show and he came in late and there was no time for a briefing and he went on cold and did the worst show of the series. The political people blamed it on the panel. Roger Ailes blamed it on the political people, saying they considered the whole business a nuisance and were making Nixon feel that way, too.

"We can't even get through to him anymore," Harry Treleaven said. "There's two groups of people in the way: one on the plane and one at headquarters and between them we can't get through. All day Thursday, Len tried to get him on the phone."

And now Murray Chotiner—*Murray Chotiner*—showed up at Fuller and Smith and Ross wanting a five-minute commercial made of an endorsement Dwight Eisenhower had given in July. A film of the endorsement was shown in the screening room. Murray Chotiner sat with his lids hanging low over his eyes. Dwight Eisenhower was wearing pajamas and lying in bed and they had put a microphone around his neck. He was a very sick man.

"No," Harry Treleaven said. "That's one thing I'm not going to do. I'm not going to make a commercial out of that."

"If you can't get five, how about at least a one-minute?" Murray Chotiner said.

"No. I'm not going to make any commercial at all."

But what Harry Treleaven and Len Garment and Frank Shakespeare would do was they would all sit down together at night and watch the Hubert Humphrey commercials or Hubert Humphrey making a speech and tell each other how terrible it was. This made them feel much better. Humphrey was such a buffoon. If he couldn't even make a decent commercial, how could he win an election? They stayed together more and more as the lead grew shorter in the polls.

THE SELLING OF THE PRESIDENT 1968

Al Scott, the assistant, came in from the road and said how depressing it was to be in New York City with all those Humphrey buttons around. And Harry Treleaven said, yes, maybe that's it. Maybe we are just feeling this way because we are in New York.

In search of some perspective, a visit was made to Arie Kopelman, who had been supervisor of the Hubert Humphrey account for Doyle, Dane, Bernbach, the advertising agency, until Doyle, Dane, Bernbach had been dismissed.

"A candidate can't be too smooth," Arie Kopelman said. "There have to be some rough edges that cling to the surface of the country and find their way into the nooks and crannies. If a communications effort is too smooth it becomes just that—a communications *effort* on the candidate's behalf rather than a projection of the candidate himself.

"Nixon is hiding behind his communications effort. Humphrey, because he doesn't have one, is out front.

"In the end, communications skills alone can't do it. I don't think it's possible to merchandise a vegetable. I think that eventually the man must show himself. If the advertising is too slick it's not then the communication of the man but the communication of the communication. Nixon's been doing the same thing for six months. There are no longer any rough edges. With Humphrey, they're not rough edges: they're grappling hooks."

Very reluctantly, Richard Nixon taped an interview with four carefully selected students on the William and Mary campus. There was nothing new, nothing stirring on the tape, but when Frank Shakespeare viewed it in New York, he said, "We've got to be very careful how we use that. Very, very selective."

It was never used at all. Like the act of talking *about* black people as anything other than crime statistics, the act of talking *to* the young—of actually being seen sitting at the same table as four students—was considered too much of a risk.

A new advertising idea was to take highlights from the panel shows and make five-minute commercials of them for use in individual states. In a highlight from Ohio, Richard Nixon was asked about foreign aid.

"Let us remember," he said. "The main purpose of American foreign aid is not to help other nations but to help ourselves."

On Thursday, October 22, the Gallup poll—considered the friendly poll by Republicans, as opposed to Harris— showed Nixon's lead in the East cut from thirteen points to five.

The *New York Daily News*, which was supporting him, showed his New York State poll lead down from four points to two. But Kevin Phillips had an explanation: "Harris does that poll for them and he deliberately used a Catholic ward in his first sample and substituted a Negro ward in his second so it would appear that a Humphrey trend was developing."

All this did not cause the Nixon people to question themselves or what they had been doing: it only made them bitter. And, from their point of view, they had a right to be. They had been technically perfect. Had accomplished everything they had set out to accomplish, from Hillsboro, New Hampshire, on up. Their efficiency had been marveled at by every observer. They were the most competent campaign organization in the history of the Republican party; perhaps the nation. They had created a climate in which Richard Nixon had been given full opportunity to expand. Simple justice demanded now that they be rewarded with what they sought—the Presidency.

This was no time for unnamed, unseen forces, antagonisms, yearnings which did not show up on radar, which could not be factored into their binary equations, to soil the record. No wonder they were bitter as well as scared. The American people had been presented with the supercandidate, the supercampaign, yet—even faced with the sweaty, babbling alternative of Humphrey—they showed signs of discontent.

◄12►

THE TAPING of the commercials in the Merv Griffin studio on October 25 marked the start of the advertising campaign's last week in New York. Afterwards, Treleaven and Al Scott walked to a Broadway restaurant called the Blue Ribbon for lunch.

"I can't get over what a great mood RN was in this morning," Scott said. "I've never seen him like that before. So relaxed."

The last of the panel shows was to be done that night, at the CBS news building on the west side. Originally, it had been intended only for New York, but with money left over and everyone getting scared, Shakespeare had decided to show it in all the big states of the East and Midwest. Whether this was good strategy or bad depended on whether you thought Richard Nixon won votes or lost them when he let people hear the things he said.

The passion for playing it safe had grown so strong that panel selection for this last show had been taken away from Roger Ailes. Shakespeare had done it himself, taking advice from Garment and Kevin Phillips.

Phillips came into the control room shortly before the show and announced that the panel was "perfectly ethnically weighted." He had prepared a chart which gave the name, sex, age, occupation, social class, nationality, and political leaning of each member. By his count, there were two "conservatives," two "moderate conservatives," one "moderate," and one "liberal." Which was an interesting count because he considered Barry Goldwater moderate.

The "moderate" for this show was a fifty-year-old Italian Catholic businessman from New Jersey. The "liberal," of course, was a Negro. Combining two categories again. A middle-aged New York banker Negro. The press representative, among all the men of reputation who could have been chosen in New York State, was someone named Gene Spagnoli of the *New York Daily News*.

"I think he's a hockey writer," Roger Ailes said.

Ailes was unhappy. "This is the worst panel we've had," he said. He cared. He had taken the programs seriously, even firing his director who could not get the close-ups, and directing the most recent five shows himself. Now, for the last and biggest, they brought in Kevin Phillips to pick the panel.

Ailes also was unhappy about Shakespeare's second-guessing of his direction during the shows. "What does he know about directing?" Ailes said. "At CBS, for Christ's sakes, he was a salesman. If he tries it tonight, I swear to God I'll turn around right in the middle of the show and take the goddamned earphones off and he can direct the son of a bitch himself."

Len Garment came into the control room.

"You up for it, Len?" someone asked.

"Ah, you've seen one show you've seen 'em all." Garment, at least, could still laugh about Spiro Agnew.

Dwight Chapin, the personal aide, who had been carrying Richard Nixon's overcoat since New Hampshire, came into the control booth to watch the show. His hair was freshly cut and there was considerable white space above his ears. He stared at the monitor, transfixed.

Nixon gave one of the standard answers he had given five hundred times since January. The studio audience applauded. And Dwight Chapin, standing in the control booth, eyes focused unblinkingly on the image of Richard Nixon on the screen, lifted his hands from his sides and slowly, softly, so as not to disturb, began to clap. He did it—as a reflex—for each answer that Richard Nixon gave.

The Negro said to Richard Nixon that it seemed curious to have so much talk of law and order now when there had been so little during the 1920s and '30s, when the Ku Klux Klan had been killing black men for sport.

Richard Nixon said it certainly was a shame what had happened to black men back then but surely, Mister So and So, you must recognize that no one suffers more from crime today than the Negro himself. And at a time when crime is rising nine times as fast as the population . . . why in another generation, Nixon seemed to say, if we didn't watch out, we'd all be criminals.

Roger Ailes was searching, somewhat desperately, for good reaction shots.

"Show me Rockefeller," he said. One of the cameras found Nelson Rockefeller in his seat. He was perfectly still, eyes half shut. Nixon finished an answer. The audience applauded. Rockefeller did not move. Not even an eyebrow.

"Somebody wake him up," Ailes said.

He looked elsewhere for reaction. To Julie, to Tricia, to John Volpe, the governor of Massachusetts. But this was the tenth panel show, the last week of the campaign.

"Wake up somebody, please," Roger Ailes said.

"I'd like to stand here and say 'send in the Marines,'" Richard Nixon was saying. "We could take out North Korea in an afternoon." But then there was the catch. "Those eighty-three men would be dead."

The Negro asked about the poverty of the rural black. Specifically in the Delta region of Mississippi.

"Well," Richard Nixon said, "your problem down there in the Delta region . . ." *Your* problem. It was always *your* problem when Negroes were involved.

"He's not a bigot," Roger Ailes once claimed. "He's just naive."

"I'm confused, sir," the Negro said, and the New York panel show, the last of the panel shows, was over.

"I didn't like that school question," Richard Nixon said afterwards, in his dressing room. "I could've gotten screwed on that."

Two things happened Sunday: Richard Nixon went on Face the Nation, and a half-hour interview, conducted by the same man who had done Spiro Agnew at Mission Bay, was shown in prime time that night.

Nixon did Face the Nation because he was getting scared. It was felt he would be hurt less by an appearance than by another flurry of excuses.

The highlight of the Sunday night show was when Nixon said his happiest memory of boyhood was one Fourth of July when all the other children had firecrackers but because his parents were so poor he could not afford them and instead he stayed indoors with his family and ate ice cream. The table, he said, was covered with a cloth on which his mother had sewn red, white, and blue bunting.

"He didn't hurt himself," Al Scott said Monday morning about Face the Nation. "That's the important thing."

But Scott was unhappy about the way Nixon had looked. "The camera height was wrong, I didn't like the chair, and there was a bad shot of the back of his head which made it look like he had a point there."

Scott promised that Meet the Press, which would be undertaken the following Sunday, would be better. "I've got a lot of friends at NBC," he said. "I can get things done without having to go to the producer and ask for changes. Sort of through the back door."

George Bush, Harry Treleaven's first client, called Monday afternoon to say that while he had not seen the Sunday night show himself, he had gotten calls asking, "What was that terrible show you had on last night for Nixon?"

"I'm trying to warm the man up, George, understand?" Harry Treleaven said. "Sort of a warm image."

He hung up shaking his head. All these great plans he had conceived through the summer did not seem to be working out. The primary campaign had been fine. There had been no interference: there had been cooperation from Nixon himself. Now things were very, very different. John Mitchell was in charge. One morning in October Harry Treleaven had to leave his office and go to a barber shop because Mitchell was coming that afternoon to look at commercials, and Treleaven said, "I don't want him to see me again without a haircut."

Meanwhile, the new advertising men who worked for Hubert Humphrey had produced a half-hour film called The Mind Changer. It was awful in many ways. It showed Hubert Humphrey and Edmund Muskie crawling down a bowling alley in their shirt sleeves. It showed Humphrey wearing a stupid fisherman's hat and getting his lines snarled on a lake near his home and it took shameless advantage of the fact he has a mentally retarded grand daughter. It was contrived and tasteless. But it was the most effective single piece of advertising of the campaign.

It showed Hubert Humphrey as a person. It began with the assumption that of course he had faults as a politician and of course he had made a lot of mistakes, but it said again and again that Hubert Humphrey, at least, is a person. Here he is sweating, laughing, crying, out in the open air. The contrast with Nixon was obvious. Nixon, who depended on a television studio the way a polio victim relied on an iron lung.

That one Humphrey film made a mockery of Richard Nixon's year-long quest for warmth. You can't create humanity, it said. You either have it or you don't. Hubert Humphrey has it. Guess who does not.

We were close to the end of this painful and difficult year and the urge was powerful to reach out to a man who cared. *The Mind Changer* matched Hubert Humphrey's heart against Richard Nixon's skills and the heart seemed by far the more appealing. The Gene Jones material had slickness, modern effect, and showed technical proficiency. But that is all the finished product said. Look, it said, here is slickness, modern effect, technical proficiency. The message was impersonal as befit Richard Nixon, who was such an impersonal man.

The Mind Changer did not look it but it was a work of genius, simply because it worked. It did not call attention to itself. One did not turn it off saying, "My, what an interesting commercial," the way one might with the Gene Jones things.

No, you turned off *The Mind Changer* and you talked about Hubert Humphrey.

On Monday night of the final week, a Democratic convention spot made by Gene Jones was shown on Laugh-In.

VIDEO	AUDIO
2. OPEN WS DEMO CONVENTION AND ZOOM IN TO SCENES OF ARGUMENT INTERCUT WITH HUMPHREY AT PODIUM.	MUSIC UP FULL: "HOT TIME IN THE OLD TOWN TONIGHT."
3. DOLLY IN ON FLAMING RIOTS IN STREETS AND SHOUTING CITIZENS.	MUSIC DISTORTED.
4. PB TO DISTURBED HUMPHREY. CUT TO MS CONVENTION AS PEOPLE WAVE FLAG. BACK TO HUMPHREY. ZOOM IN AS SCREEN SHAKES.	MUSIC UP FULL: "HOT TIME."
5. SCREEN SHAKES AS TWO GI's CROUCH BESIDE BUNKER UNDER FIRE IN RVN. MONTAGE OF SHOTS OF MEN IN AID STATION, THEIR FACES TENSE UNDER FIRE. PAN ACROSS BLASTED LAND LITTERED WITH EXPENDED SHELL CASINGS.	MUSIC WARPED.
6. SLOW DISSOLVE IN ON MCU OF HUMPHREY. HOLD.	MUSIC UP FULL "HOT TIME."

VIDEO	AUDIO
7. ZOOM IN ON POOR FARMER IN APPALACHIA STANDING ON PORCH OF HIS HOME. INTERCUTS OF POOR WOMAN AND HUNGRY CHILD AT TABLE AND SMALL GIRL PEERING OUT WINDOW OF HER CABIN.	MUSIC DISTORTED.
8. SLOW ZOOM IN ON HUMPHREY. AS THE CAMERA TAKES HIM FULL FACE PRISMATIC LENS CREATES THREE HUMPHREY FACES FILLING THE SCREEN. HOLD.	MUSIC UP FULL: "HOT TIME IN THE OLD TOWN TONIGHT." MUSIC OUT.

9. FADEOUT.

It was a stark and jarring sixty seconds. By far Richard Nixon's toughest commercial of the campaign. Still, it probably would not have attracted attention except for element number six in the script. This was a close-up of Hubert Humphrey laughing. Coming right after the scene of the soldiers crouching by their bunkers, it gave the undeniable impression that Humphrey was laughing at them.

Immediately, so the newspapers said the next day, the NBC switchboard was flooded with protest calls. Frank Shakespeare said the calls were phony, a Democratic plot engineered by Larry O'Brien. If so, it was a good one.

The New York Times sent a man to Fuller and Smith and Ross the next day to ask how and why the commercial had been produced. The reporter spoke to a vice president named Dick DePew. What an opportunity this was for DePew. For almost six months Harry Treleaven had been rubbing their noses in it at Fuller and Smith and Ross and now there was trouble and Dick DePew knew exactly what to do.

DePew told the man that no one from Fuller and Smith and Ross had even seen the spot, much less created it. It had all been the work of a man named Treleaven, and his office was just down the hall.

DePew did not stop there. He also told the man from the *Times* that this was one of the most reprehensible examples of unethical advertising he had ever seen.

"They tried a smear and it didn't work," DePew said.

The *Times*, delighted to find such remarks attributable to a member of Nixon's own agency, took great pains not to underplay the story.

Harry Treleaven did not want to talk about it. "A craven cop out," was all he would say.

"I'd throw that son of a bitch DePew out a window," Charley Garment said, "except he might land on a Republican."

Fuller and Smith and Ross took a quick survey of reaction to the spot. They found no one very angry, which made Shakespeare more certain than ever that the phone calls had been faked and that the papers had played up the story simply to embarrass Nixon. Some viewers, according to Fuller and Smith and Ross, thought the spot had been a Humphrey commercial. Others thought it was just another part of the Laugh-In show.

The next day, the *New York Daily News* poll showed that Humphrey had gained seven points in three days to lead Nixon by 4.2 points in New York State. Kevin Phillips was running out of excluded Catholics to explain it.

◀13▶

LEN GARMENT walked to the newsstand in the TWA terminal at Kennedy airport and bought *Time*, *Harper's*, and the weekend edition of the *New York Post*. Then he went upstairs to the snack shop to have a cup of coffee. By this time, Garment was well conditioned. He immediately opened the newspaper and started to look for the ads. The first was on page sixty-four. It filled the page.

"The Truth Hurts at Times," the top line said. Harry Treleaven had written it. He had intended it as a pun. Then the ad went into small print that ran on for twelve paragraphs explaining how *The New York Times* had been wrong and unfair in the things it had said about Spiro Agnew in an editorial one week before. The editorial had implied that Agnew used his position as governor of Maryland to make money on the side. The ad said how this was not true, and then quoted such other papers as the *Washington Post*, the *Washington Star*, the *Baltimore Sun*, and the *St. Louis Globe-Democrat* as defending Agnew. Then there was a picture of Agnew and a quote in which he called the *Times* editorial "libel," and then the bottom line, which said, "In their search for truth, men must rise above the Times!"

Harry Treleaven had spent most of his last two days in New York preparing the ad, which would run in the *Times* on Monday. "It was something Nixon himself wanted done," Treleaven said. "And even if it doesn't get us any votes, it's worth it just for the fun of hitting those guys."

Len Garment turned to page seventy-eight. Here there was a half-page ad. The top line said only, "Tuesday."

Below that it continued:

It will be quiet on Tuesday.

No speeches. No motorcades. No paid political announcements. It's a very special day, just for grown-ups.

America votes Tuesday.

We'll vote for one of three middle-aged men, all ordinary enough looking, each with a set of mannerisms and beliefs and strengths and weaknesses.

And we're not doing anybody any favors when we choose him. It's a terrible job.

Our choice isn't difficult. There is no choice.

We believe the Democratic candidate is a decent man, trapped between 1932 and Camelot. And at a time when this nation cries for unity, he talks in the sad, old jargon of the hyphenated American—Spanish-American, Black-American, Old-American, Young-American, Businessman-American, Union member-American.

We must stop talking to Americans as special interest groups and start talking to special interest groups as Americans.

We looked at the Third Party candidate, and we were told that he was "courageous." But courage without grace is meanness. And there's more than a dime's worth of difference between courage and meanness.

We're going to vote for Richard Nixon.

His years of high office, his moments of defeat, and the vital—almost forgotten—rest from the pace of public life have blended into a mature judgment this nation desperately needs.

We choose Mr. Nixon with the full knowledge that America will not live happily ever after November 5th. The next four years will test this nation's belief in itself more than any other period in its history.

On Tuesday, the shouting and the begging and the threatening and the heckling will be silenced. It's very quiet in a voting booth.

And nobody's going to help you make up your mind. So— just for that instant—you'll know what the man you're voting for will do a thousand times a day for the next four years.

Now it's your turn.

Len Garment closed the paper.

"That's the best copy written in the whole campaign," he said.

"Who did it?"

"Some guy in California. Originally, it was just going to run out there but they sent it in for approval and when I saw it I decided it was too good to confine to one state."

The morning was sunny and warm. The terminal was not crowded. This was Saturday, November 2, and the New York tension and strain was behind. There was only the telethon remaining, in the escape world of southern California. The next time anyone saw New York it would be the evening of Election Day with the polls almost closed and the counting under way. The ad men had come a long way—new at politics, new at trying to understand a man as complicated as Richard Nixon, and unsure how to present what they felt were his virtues to a people who rejected him as a reflex.

Len Garment, like the others, was convinced there was much good beneath the surface, but the attempt to render the surface appealing—even acceptable—had been like trying to grow grass on the moon.

"What do you think, Len?"

"It looks very good," he said. "Honestly. Wallace is falling apart, the Border States are coming back. New York is going but New York has never been essential to our plans. If we do get New York it will be an avalanche. Even without it, I think we'll do all right."

He talked about the late turn in the campaign. About how so much of America, tolerant, passive, resigned to Richard Nixon for so much of the year, had suddenly gone sour.

"I don't think it's a result of anything he has done or has not done," Garment said, "but a result of Humphrey's decision to attack him personally. Which of course was the right decision from Humphrey's point of view. That, plus the liberal press stirring up the old anti-Nixon feelings."

"Then you really don't think you've been overcautious?"

Len Garment shook his head. "If we win, we'll be proven right."

Then he said, "Look, we can't shape events. All we can do is react. If it had not been for Wallace looking so strong, for instance, the choice of a vice president probably would have been different. All that was on our part was a reaction, not some burning desire to make Agnew a national figure."

Then Harry Treleaven and Ruth Jones came into the terminal and walked up the stairs. Treleaven saw Garment drinking coffee.

"The hell with this," he said. "I'm going to get a drink." He went over to the bar.

"You know, I think I could really become a drunk," Treleaven said, "if I only had the time. I love to drink but I'm always too busy."

They sat quietly in the late morning, looking down at the red carpets and the terminal concourse below.

"This is kind of a sentimental journey," Harry Treleaven said.

"Yes. Our last trip," Garment said.

They ordered a second drink.

"How do you feel, Harry? What do you think?"

"I'm at the same point now as I was two weeks ago. But I've been both ways. I'm more confident now than I was two days ago."

"Oh, by the way," Len Garment said, "we took a quick poll after the bombing pause was announced and found that ninety-seven percent of the people said it would not change their vote. Of those who said it would, two per cent went from Humphrey to Nixon, a half percent from Humphrey to undecided and a half per cent from undecided to Humphrey."

"That's surprising."

"People aren't so dumb."

"You think it was done just to help Humphrey?"

"Of course," Len Garment said.

The plane left at one o'clock. Ruth Jones told a story of how the Democratic convention spot, which had been ordered pulled from all scheduled appearances after the complaints, had got on the air the following night in Syracuse.

"That's a funny story," Harry Treleaven said.

"Oh, it's hilarious. Everyone thought so but Frank." She made a motion with her thumb toward the back of the first-class section where Frank Shakespeare was sitting.

"He didn't think it was funny at all. He was purple. He demanded that the station broadcast an apology every hour and he kept saying to me, 'Ruth, can we really be sure some little seventy-three-dollar-a-week Humphreyite didn't do it on purpose?' "

Later, I walked back to Shakespeare and Garment. Garment was reading *Harper's,* the issue with Norman Mailer's reports of the two conventions.

"You like that?" I asked.

"Fantastic. Just fantastic," he said.

Shakespeare looked up from whatever he was reading, which was not Norman Mailer.

"How many electoral votes are we going to get?" he said.

I told him I thought about three hundred.

"Low," he said. "You're too low."

"Three fifty?"

"In that range."

There was a man selling flowers on a street corner between the Los Angeles airport and Beverly Hills. Frank Shakespeare asked Harry Treleaven to stop the car. He got out and bought some flowers.

"Here," he said, and gave them to Ruth Jones.

A few minutes later he said, "Here's something: When the announcement of the bombing pause was made one of the first things we thought of was that we'd have to go through all the old panel shows which were being used again as commercials to make sure there were no outdated references. The one scheduled to run first was Texas. But when I mentioned this to RN he said, 'Texas? Oh, no, you don't have to worry about that one. There's nothing in the Texas show that will be affected.' And he was right. Isn't that amazing? All the different shows he's done and he could remember in an instant that there was no reference in the Texas show to the bombing."

Treleaven stopped first at the Century Plaza Hotel to let Garment and Shakespeare off.

"Len's really funny," Treleaven said. "He'd much rather

stay at the Beverly Hills Hotel but he's afraid to because he thinks, with Nixon staying at the Century Plaza, he should stay there, too."

"And how about Frank?"

"Frank doesn't care. Frank couldn't tell the difference."

The next day, Sunday, Richard Nixon did Meet the Press. Before the show, Roger Ailes told him to "come in under" the questioners in tone. It was agreed later that he had done very well. Several people, Ailes included, thought it had been his best TV appearance of the campaign.

After the show, Ailes drove an hour and a half north, to an airfield, where a friend had arranged for him to make his first parachute jump. He missed the landing zone on his first try and decided to jump again. The second time, he hit the landing zone but ripped ligaments in his ankle. He had to take pills for the pain that night.

It rained but in the morning it was clear. Harry Treleaven came out of the hotel at 10 A.M.

"Where are you going?" I asked.

"I've got to get Len drunk," he said. "He's *so* tense."

Roger Ailes came out of the hotel on crutches.

"How does it feel?"

"The son of a bitch hurts." He rode in a rented yellow Thunderbird over the hill to Burbank where the NBC studio was.

The studio was very big. One hundred and twenty-five telephones had been installed for the operators who would take calls during the show. The operators had been recruited by the local Republican organization. There also were seats for several hundred spectators, to be recruited by the organization, too. Richard Nixon had grown accustomed to hearing his answers applauded. It seemed foolish to deprive him on the final night of the campaign.

Roger Ailes hobbled to the front row of the audience section. Immy Fiorentino, the lighting man, who had been used for the later panel shows and the Madison Square Garden rally, was there.

"It's going to be a dull fucking two hours," Roger Ailes said. "That's for openers."

Immy Fiorentino shrugged. Dull, sparkling, he did not much care. As long as it was properly lit.

"How are these questions going to work?" he asked.

"Well, what's going to happen," Roger Ailes said, "is all of the questions are going to come through the operators over there, and then runners will bring them down to the producer's table, which will be set up here, and from there they'll go to a screening room where the Nixon staff will tear them up and write their own. Then they'll go to Bud Wilkinson who will cleverly read them and Nixon will read the answers off a card."

Later, Jack Rourke was asked how it really would work.

"I understand Paul Keyes has been sitting up for two days writing questions," Roger Ailes said.

"Well, not quite," Jack Rourke said. He seemed a little embarrassed.

"What is going to happen?"

"Oh . . ."

"It's sort of semiforgery, isn't it?" Ailes said. "Keyes has a bunch of questions Nixon wants to answer. He's written them in advance to make sure they're properly worded.

When someone calls with something similar, they'll use Keyes' question and attribute it to the person who called. Isn't that it?"

"More or less," Jack Rourke said.

At first, they were going to have Richard Nixon sit on the edge of a desk, as he had done at the Merv Griffin studio. The first desk that the NBC set designer had provided was on wheels.

"Jesus Christ, he'll lean against that and go sliding off the set," Roger Ailes said. "It will be the highlight of the campaign."

Then Frank Shakespeare called: since there were going to be two separate telethons (one for the East, one for the West); lasting two hours each, it was felt that the edge of the desk would tend to be uncomfortable. Nixon preferred a "comfortable black swivel chair." Roger Ailes told the set designer to produce one.

Then Ailes hobbled through the studio again, trying to develop a feel for it. Some sense that would enable him to infuse the program, somehow, with imagination. To give originality and élan to what seemed doomed to tedium.

"If we put Julie and Tricia over there, answering phones, we have to be careful who we put around them." He turned to an assistant. "Dolores, make a note of that. Make sure we get good-looking girls around Julie and Tricia."

He talked to the cameramen. "Sixty, sixty-five, seventy percent of the show will be RN on camera talking. You've got to watch him—I like to shoot him close but two hours on stage and he's going to perspire. So get away from him every once in a while and let him mop."

"Do you want Kleenex on stage?" a floor man asked.

"No, he'll have a handkerchief in his inside breast pocket."

In the control room, most attention centered around the splicing of a Jackie Gleason endorsement which was going into the beginning of the show. Gleason had made the tape in Miami and it had been used first at the start of the Madison Square Garden rally: "*My name is Jackie Gleason and I love this country. I've never made a public choice like this before—but I think this country needs Dick Nixon and we need him now.*"

Paul Keyes had written the words. He was turning out to be a very useful, if unofficial, addition to the campaign staff.

Roger Ailes had his right ankle in a bucket of ice.

"Jesus Christ, this hurts," he said. "Dolores, give me another of those pills, will you? I wish there were some way to pipe the Humphrey thing in here tonight. It will be a hell of a lot more interesting."

Ailes was in bad pain. And tired. And facing four hours of live direction in the evening. And—as the only member of Richard Nixon's staff who would have thought to jump from an airplane the day before the biggest TV production of the campaign—feeling quite alone. He sat with his foot in an ice bucket in the control room through the afternoon, wishing he were done and in Grenada, where he was going on vacation later in the week.

Frank Shakespeare and Paul Keyes got to the studio at three o'clock. Shakespeare was in his standard dark suit, Keyes in a sky blue turtleneck. Ailes struggled out to meet them.

"Watch," he said. "Now they'll rip the whole thing up and start again."

The first change Shakespeare made was moving Julie and Tricia up from the second row to the first. Ailes had wanted them in the second row to make them seem simply part of the crowd, but Shakespeare said Nixon wanted to greet them as he entered and it would be awkward to have him leaning over other girls.

"And then he'll walk over," Shakespeare was saying, "and when he greets them I think he should kiss them."

"Well, I think kissing is a bit much," Paul Keyes said.

"But if he comes over, he's got to kiss them."

"No, it looks stagy," Keyes said. "We'll have him go right to his chair."

"Have him kiss one of the other broads," Ailes said.

Paul Keyes continued to check the set. "Roger, can you put that camera one in closer so RN will be physically conscious of it?"

Ailes explained why moving the camera would be a problem.

"I know that," Keyes said. "But this was the one specific thing he asked for this morning. That we give him a camera close enough so he would be physically conscious of it. He wants this to be a very intimate show between him and the American people. And the only way he can do it is if that camera is right on top of him."

Ailes explained more of the technical problems.

"But RN wants to *converse* tonight. Low key, easy, informal. He doesn't want to make a speech. And he needs the camera there to push him into the low key."

Ailes rearranged the cameras.

"Okay," Paul Keyes said, "now, can four come in a little closer?"

"Yeah, but if I bring four in—"

"He needs it close, Roger."

"Okay. You position four where you want it and I'll re-stage."

Paul Keyes stared at the cameras.

"Is four better than the crane camera?" Roger Ailes said.

"Yes. For his needs tonight."

"Then the crane is dead. We don't even need it. But that means we can't get a shot of Wilkinson at all because to take it we have to take the other camera. See, the best shot of RN is in the crane but if that's not close enough to give the effect he needs, we won't use it."

"I know it's a problem," Paul Keyes said. "But he needs the camera up close. He'll be talking to the camera, not to Bud. He wants to go into the living room."

Finally, Ailes found a way to move the crane camera in over Bud Wilkinson's shoulder and provide the "physical presence" Richard Nixon needed.

"Perfect," Paul Keyes said. "I know that will do it for him."

"Of course that kills my opening shot completely," Ailes said. "It's also going to kill the shot of the audience on one."

But Keyes was not concerned with this. "That camera might as well be Wilkinson to the Old Man," he was saying.

"But if the crane has to be in that close you're never going to get Wilkinson in the foreground. You'll never see the relationship between the two men. Does it have to be that close?"

"It has to be close, Roger. How far back would you want it?"

"I need another two feet."

"Two feet, okay. If that will serve your purposes we can compromise. But it can't go out any further."

"It's almost not worth the compromise. Frankly, it's not that great a shot. . . . Wait a minute, is four any good or is that too far away?"

"Four is perfect. The important thing is the relationship between him and the camera. He needs that nearness."

"Okay," Roger Ailes said, and told the floor manager to mark with tape how far forward and to the left camera four could go without moving into the range of any of the other cameras.

"Just tell RN he'll have that one camera he can play to and we'll screw around with the others," Roger Ailes said, and the problem was solved.

Paul Keyes sat in the chair that had been brought out for Richard Nixon.

"It's too loose. It's got to have a solid back to it."

"Okay, I'll take care of that," Roger Ailes said, and he went slowly back to the control room and called the set designer and told him they needed another chair. The designer protested.

"Do you want him to tip over?" Ailes said. "The back is loose. Do you want him to lean back and go over on his ass?"

The designer suggested using an orange chair he had brought out earlier.

"Goddamn it, no, we're not going to use an orange chair. We've been through that . . . I said we're not going to use an orange chair . . . well, fuck it, then. Forget it. I'll get the goddamn chair." He put down the phone and turned to Dolores Hardie, the assistant.

"Get Bob Dwan to get a goddamn chair. I told that creepy bastard of a designer as soon as he brought it out that we weren't going to use an orange chair."

It was four o'clock in the afternoon. Frank Shakespeare was worried about the studio getting too hot.

"Make sure you've got that handkerchief soaked in witch hazel," Roger Ailes told someone. "I can't do that sincerity bit with the camera if he's sweating."

Shakespeare got more worried about the temperature. "He's going to be out there four hours tonight."

It was decided to cancel the five o'clock rehearsal of the opening so the lights could be shut off, the studio sealed, and cold air piped in. Roger Ailes went across the hall to a dressing room and lay down on a couch.

"This is the beginning of a whole new concept," Ailes said. "This is it. This is the way they'll be elected forevermore. The next guys up will have to be performers.

"The interesting question is, how sincere is a TV set? If you take a cold guy and stage him warm, can you get away with it? I don't know. But I felt a lot better about jumping out of that plane yesterday than I do about this thing tonight."

The announcer who was to do the opening called to ask if his tone was too shrill.

"Yeah, we don't want it like a quiz show," Roger Ailes said. "He's going to be presidential tonight so announce presidentially."

The studio was opened and the hundred and twenty-five girls who had volunteered to answer the phones were led in. Frank Shakespeare watched them take their places and an expression of horror came over his face.

"Oh my God!" he said. "This is terrible! Where are the black faces? Where are the black faces?"

He turned and went running off to find the woman who was in charge of the volunteers. She was a heavy woman with gray hair.

"We're going live across the country on Election Eve in an hour and a half and there's not one black face up there. We can't do that. It looks terrible."

"I know," the woman said. "I know. We tried. In fact we had twenty who agreed to come. But none of them showed up."

"This is terrible," Shakespeare said.

The woman gave a shrug that said, What do you expect me to do? After all, you know they're undependable.

There was one Negro girl, sitting near the end of the next-to-last row. Someone pointed her out to Shakespeare.

"Oh, yeah," he said. Staring.

"I could ask her to come down front so you'd be sure to get her in the picture."

Shakespeare never faltered. "Would you? Gee, that would be terrific. Terrific."

The Hubert Humphrey telethon, which started half an hour before Nixon's, was being shown in the press room. Humphrey was on with Paul Newman, Buddy Hackett, Danny Thomas and others. He was obsequious to them all. Cue cards, other cameras, and a morass of wires and unused folding chairs were visible all over the stage. The Humphrey producers, apparently, had left their shirttails out on purpose; to point up the contrast with what they considered the contrived slickness of Nixon.

More startling, Humphrey was answering questions live. Actually talking to the people who called on the phone. There was no Paul Keyes, no Bud Wilkinson to protect him.

"That's crazy," Al Scott said, appalled at what he saw. "They've got no control."

Richard Nixon was in a good mood. He sat in his comfortable black swivel chair with the back that had been tightened, his legs crossed, his smile seeming less forced than usual, his voice and rhetoric pleasantly subdued. If camera four had been any closer it would have put out his eye.

He leaned into it as Bud Wilkinson read each question and

responded in his most conversational tone. The substance was no different from what it had been all along, but the style was at its peak. The social security question was repeated at the beginning of each hour—on both shows—so that anyone who had just tuned in would be sure to hear that Richard Nixon did not intend to have senior citizens forming bread lines in the streets.

Paul Keyes had added a few twists to break the monotony of the answers. At one point, Bud Wilkinson walked across the room to where Julie and Tricia were answering phones and asked them what seemed to be on most callers' minds. Then David Eisenhower read a letter from his grandfather. Earnestly. Then there was the chat with Mrs. Nixon.

She answered a couple of Wilkinson/Paul Keyes questions of less than monumental importance, and then, as the audience—on cue—applauded, she grinned and . . . began to applaud herself.

It was simply a reflex. There had been so much applause in her life. Going all the way back to the days of Beauty and the Beast. And all through this campaign. She had sat, half-listening, then with her mind drifting more and more as the weeks and speeches passed so slowly into one another. Bringing her finally to this television studio on this final night where all that was left of her was reflex: you hear applause—applaud.

Then, in a cruel instant, she realized what she had done and that no doubt her error had been communicated to the nation by those evil black cameras she had learned to dread. Here, on the last night, with everything fitting neatly into place as it had from the start, she had spoiled it.

She jerked her hands up to cover her face. Roger Ailes switched quickly to another shot.

Other than that, the two hours went smoothly, though

after the immense effort of preparation it was inconceivable that they could have gone any other way. All along, whatever else the campaign was not, it was smooth.

Between shows, Richard Nixon disappeared into a dressing room for a ham and cheese sandwhich, a cup of coffee, a shower, a rubdown, and a clean shirt.

David Eisenhower, looking tall and bewildered, wandered down from his seat. He was carrying two colored photographs of Richard Nixon. He approached Jack Rourke.

"Do you suppose I could get these autographed?" he said.

"You know him as well as I do," Jack Rourke said.

"Yeah," David Eisenhower said. He walked away slowly. Then he saw Dwight Chapin. He repeated his request.

"Now?" Chapin asked, straining to believe what he was hearing. "You want those autographed now?"

David Eisenhower managed a tentative nod.

"Oh, no," Dwight Chapin said. "Not now."

Richard Nixon tired a bit during the second show and started talking about those hundreds of confessed murderers who had been set free by the Supreme Court, but it was not noticeable enough to prevent Frank Shakespeare from patting people on the shoulder in the control booth and saying, "He's strong. He's strong."

Toward the end, Bud Wilkinson began a question by saying, "This one is from a carpenter named Bob Will in Orlando, Florida . . ."

And Richard Nixon started his answer with, "Well, you see, Mr. Carpenter . . ."

But the campaign was over.

"I'm not a showman," Richard Nixon was telling America. "I'm not a television personality."

Afterwards, Paul Keyes strode down the building's main corridor. "Perfect! Perfect! He did it just like he said he was going to. He said it was nice guy time tonight. He said he wasn't going to go for punch lines. He wasn't going to go for applause. Just come in low and thoughtful. And he did it!"

Roger Ailes was helped down the stairway and out to the car.

"Tonight," he said, "this was the Nixon I met on the Douglas show. This was the Nixon I wanted to work for."

◄14►

H<small>ARRY</small> T<small>RELEAVEN</small> was eating breakfast, alone, in the room called the Loggia at the Beverly Hills Hotel. It was seven-thirty. The sun already was very bright. The room, its tables covered by pink, looked just as it had in July. Harry Treleaven looked older.

"It's going to be tight," he said.

"Does that mean you're less confident now than you were two days ago?"

"It's going to be tight," he repeated.

The final Harris poll, released the day before, had put Humphrey ahead for the first time of the campaign. Frank Shakespeare, who had claimed all along that the Harris poll was rigged, was threatening an investigation if Nixon won.

Treleaven finished his breakfast and went to his room for his bag. Ruth Jones came to the table. She had been up until four o'clock in the morning, buying radio time for an Election Night spot which would have David Eisenhower reading the letter from his grandfather the same way he had on the Telethon. Everyone thought the Telethon had been fine. But everyone was scared.

By eight o'clock we were out of the hotel, moving toward the airport in the heavy morning traffic. A man on the car radio said that the first signs of concern had begun to show up among the Nixon staff, which, he said, until a day or two before, had been almost infuriating with its smugness. Harry Treleaven laughed.

The plane took off at nine o'clock. The stewardess passed out plastic glasses of champagne that was sweet and warm. Treleaven drank his and then mine. He was trying to relax. It was hard, after a year of eighteen-hour days, to suddenly have nothing to do. There would be no calls to make when the plane landed, no meetings to rush to in a cab. It was done. Now there was only the wait.

"There was a lot we didn't do because we didn't think we had to," Treleaven said. "The big lead influenced our whole approach.

"Then we had the basic problem of Nixon's personality. There were certain things people just would not buy about the guy. For instance, he loves to walk on the beach, but we couldn't send a camera out to film him picking up seashells. That would not have been credible."

He was already looking for reasons why things had gone wrong. There was no question anymore about whether they had or not. The perfect campaign, the computer campaign, the technicians' campaign, the television campaign, the one that would make them rewrite the textbooks had collapsed beneath the weight of Nixon's grayness.

"That total split between the advertising and political people was very bad," Treleaven said. "It left us much less effective than we could have been."

And then, Harry Treleaven said, there had been Spiro Agnew. "More than any other single thing," he said, "I think that damaged the image we were trying to build."

He shook his head in bewilderment. One thing about advertising cigarettes or airplanes: they don't resist.

New York was gray as the plane came down. The artificial

music came into the cabin as it landed. The song was familiar: *"Try to remember, a day in September . . ."*

"Hear that song, Harry? You think they're trying to tell you something?"

"I hope not," Treleaven said. His mouth was tight again. He was twisting his neck nervously beneath his collar.

I checked into Al Scott's room at the Waldorf-Astoria, Nixon's Election night headquarters, at seven-thirty. Scott had stopped at his apartment before coming to the hotel. I ordered a grilled cheese and bacon sandwich from room service. It took over an hour to get there and they forgot the bacon. I turned on the television set. CBS said it looked like Indiana would go to Humphrey. None of it was real anymore.

Roger Ailes had a room four flights above. I called him. His wife was with him so I did not go up.

"Coming back on the plane, RN said the key state was Connecticut," Ailes said. "He said if we win there we've got it big, but if we lose that one we're in trouble."

I hung up and watched the television again. CBS admitted they had been wrong about Indiana but then they put a big check up next to Humphrey's name in Connecticut and said he would carry the state with something like 65 per cent of the vote. I called Ailes again.

"If he does lose," Ailes said, "and he has any sense of humor, the first thing he'll say when he comes out to concede is, 'Well, gentlemen, you won't have Nixon to kick around anymore.'"

I went downstairs to the ballroom on the third floor but it was full of out-of-town Republicans, police, and cigarette smoke. There was no sign of Harry Treleaven, Shakespeare, Garment, or anyone. I went back to the room.

Al Scott showed up, dropped off his coat, went downstairs, came back an hour later, said, "It looks hairy," picked up his coat and went home. The advertising work was done. This night was for the politicians.

It would be either Nixon or the House of Representatives. I fell asleep.

I woke up in the fuzzy early morning and someone on the television said it had all come down to Illinois. I remembered then the decision they made in Key Biscayne to cut the budget for Illinois because they were so far ahead. I made a mental note to ask Kevin Phillips what had happened. If I ever saw Kevin Phillips again. Then I fell back asleep.

When I woke up again it was light out and they were saying Nixon had won. Perhaps there was something in Richard Daley's moral code that would not let him steal the Presidency from the same man twice.

I called Ailes, whose wife had left early in the morning, and we decided to go up to the thirty-fifth floor where Nixon was. The lobby of the suite was done in gold, with cream colored rugs. Richard Nixon was President-elect. The atmosphere was very restrained. Ladies with gray hair and colorless dresses sat in one huge room, sipping coffee and tea. All the men were shaved and wore freshly pressed suits.

Billy Graham, whose suit was not only pressed but expensive, came breezing past, an overcoat slung over his arm.

"We did it," he said, grinning, his blond hair neatly waved. He went directly to Nixon's room, without explaining whether "we" meant Billy Graham and Richard Nixon or Billy Graham and God or perhaps all three together.

Len Garment was standing in a doorway.

"Congratulations," I said.

He smiled. He had started with it, full-time, before any of

the others. Back when there was no headquarters, no $21 million budget, no Billy Graham in the suite. Just a couple of guys in a law firm who decided to help their boss.

Ailes and I stayed a little longer and then went down to the ballroom where Nixon would make his first appearance as President-elect. We watched from a balcony, Ailes sweating with the pain of his ankle, and when it was over I went down to the bar.

Jimmy Breslin, Murray Kempton, and Bill Barry, who had been bodyguard to Bobby Kennedy in his campaign, were having a sad drink together.

Kempton had written a column that morning, which began, "We are two nations of equal size. . . . Richard Nixon's nation is white, Protestant, breathes clean air and advances toward middle-age. Hubert Humphrey's nation is everything else, whatever is black, most of which breathes polluted air, pretty much what is young. . . .

"There seems no place larger than Peoria from which [Nixon] has not been beaten back; he is the President of every place in this country which does not have a bookstore. . . ."

Bill Barry finished his drink and left. This day was almost too much for him to bear.

Breslin was talking of leaving the country. Moving to Ireland. It seemed an appealing idea.

"That's a marvelous commentary on the progress of the twentieth century," Murray Kempton said. "Joyce begins it by leaving Ireland to be free and Breslin ends it by going back."

‹15›

THE NEXT DAY it poured rain. It was also very cold. Harry Treleaven got to his office in the morning and began to pack.

Among the papers on his desk was a blue folder which had lain there for several weeks. The folder had a cover of clear plastic. On the cover there was one word: TRANSITION. The folder had been prepared by Eugene Jones. Inside, the word TRANSITION was repeated and under it was the line: "A color television special one hour in length."

Then there was the description and the outline:

To be seen in prime time on a major network during the Sunday evening of the weekend prior to the Inauguration of Richard M. Nixon as 37th President of the United States.

It will be narrated by Alistair Cooke and Bob Hope.

The theme is based on the public's increasing anticipation of change between the Johnson and Nixon administrations. A reiteration of the necessity for this change and the manner in which President-Elect Nixon intends to execute it is the heartbeat of the program.

Entirely a color presentation, it is composed essentially of film-motion picture and animated stills—with a special video tape sequence of approximately six minutes in length near the program's end.

Production is to commence one week prior to November 5th and terminate in the latter part of January. The program will be created by ESJ Productions, Inc. A large unit will be assembled, composed of the best technicians, writers, musicians and others required for this special project. Camera crews are to be involved in special coverage throughout this country and certain areas abroad. Eugene S. Jones personally will produce and direct. Overall production budget is $575,000.

SOME IMPORTANT ELEMENTS

1. THE BEGINNING—A mandate on Election Day.
    A. The people vote.
    B. The world watches on global TV.
    C. Drama and excitement of Election Eve. Intercuts from perspectives of the giant NBC studios to the private Nixon suite.
    D. Nixon the victor—the concession—the candidate, now President-elect, at a time of high tide.
2. THE JOURNEY—New Hampshire—Miami—the campaign.
    A. The need for change.
    B. The great issues—order, Vietnam, poverty, etc.
    C. The creation of a new bridge of real communication between people and government.
3. THE NIXON TRANSITION—An introduction to tomorrow.
    A. The new government—cabinet appointees and others filmed in the reality environments which relate to their new roles. They talk—on the move—in cinema verité —already in action.
    B. The process of orderly change from one administration

to another. How the national interests are protected and served.

C. A revealing insight into the awesome complexity and responsibilities of the Nixon Presidency.

4. THE MOLDING OF A PRESIDENT—The background story.

A. A different kind of biographical portrait which illuminates the personal story of Dick Nixon from those formative years in Whittier up through his marriage to Pat and service in the South Pacific during World War II. Illustrated with still photos and rare footage.

B. Special insert narrative for the above will come from actual remembrances recorded all over the United States with men and women who:

—shared the childhood years with R.N.

—were his boyhood chums or fellow students.

—served in combat with him.

—recall his courtship of Pat.

—early on were aware of this young lawyer's dedication to public service.

5. FACE TO FACE—President-Elect Nixon talks to America.

A. Thanks for the vote of confidence.

B. His plans—his determination.

C. A firm expression of hope—a world which above all seeks peace.

D. The Nixon family joins the President-Elect on camera.

6. SUMMING UP.

A. Very short.

B. Upbeat, positive, inspirational.

That was a bit too much, even for the image builders. Instead, Frank Shakespeare produced a half-hour program on which Richard Nixon introduced the members of his cabinet. But the idea was the same. Keep the people on the other side of the screen. And Richard Nixon, even though he had not liked the process, had learned. He began to hold televised press conferences at which he used no notes, not even a podium. Just like the panel show except the questions were a little more intelligent.

Harry Treleaven walked around a corner to a small screening room and asked a projectionist to show a reel that contained commercials from the primary campaign. He had developed an almost sentimental attachment to the memory of those days. When Richard Nixon had listened. When no one interfered.

There were several spots in which Nixon talked to small groups of citizens. These were the forerunners of the panel shows.

There was one, made in Oregon, in which Nixon was asked what he thought about this whole business of image.

"People are much less impressed with image arguments than are columnists, commentators, and pollsters," he said. "And I for one rejected the advice of the public relations experts who say that I've got to sit by the hour and watch myself. The American people may not like my face but they're going to listen to what I have to say."

Harry Treleaven smiled.

"I don't know why I enjoy that," he said. "But I do."

◄APPENDIX►

"Nowadays everybody tells us that what we need is more belief, a stronger and deeper and more encompassing faith. A faith in America and in what we are doing. That may be true in the long run. What we need first and now is to disillusion ourselves. What ails us most is not what we have done with America, but what we have substituted for America. We suffer primarily not from our vices or our weaknesses, but from our illusions. We are haunted, not by reality, but by those images we have put in place of reality."

—Daniel Boorstin, *The Image*

Notes re Nixon for President Advertising in the Primary Campaigns

HARRY TRELEAVEN

November 21, 1967

Consider this the first stab at an advertising strategy—a combination guide and thought-starter for those who will be developing the Nixon for President advertising in the primary states.

Much that is in these notes has been said before. Some of the points are obvious. A few are less obvious and perhaps new. But all have a direct bearing on our problem and merit your close study.

There is nothing final about this document. It is a beginning only. Like Alaskan sourdough, it should be constantly kneaded with fresh ideas for best results.

We must start by answering three questions which are basic to all advertising:

—*What* do we want to communicate? This is the most important question. And once answered, *all* advertising should carry the same message, and be judged solely on how clearly and memorably it communicates it.

—*How* do we say what we want to communicate? With what words, what audio and visual techniques, in what style, what tone of voice?

—*Where* should we put our advertising message so that it will reach the most voters in the most effective way possible at the least cost? This is the media decision, and because it is a local problem it will be the subject of individual reports for each state.

The content, or the "what," of the advertising

We must keep foremost in our minds the fact that we are developing advertising for a *primary* campaign. LBJ and the Democratic Party are not yet the opposition. Criticizing the present administration is merely a way—and a good one, to be sure—to present our candidate as the Republican most qualified to head a new administration.

Thus, the overall objective of the advertising will be to persuade voters, or confirm to the already-persuaded, that the Republican nominee in 1968 should be Richard Nixon, rather than Romney or Rockefeller or Reagan or Percy.

Issues will be discussed, but always in a way that clearly establishes Richard Nixon as the Republican candidate who is best equipped to deal with them.

And the advertising will certainly attack the record and policies of the administration. As the McDonald Davis Schmidt strategy states, "The most effective posture for a challenger to take is that of constantly challenging. The advertising should be directed toward 'what's wrong with things as they are.'" True. But it must always then lead directly, and without subtlety, into why our candidate is so uniquely qualified to right those wrongs.

It is part of the discipline of sound advertising to put down, as briefly as possible, the advertising "proposition"—the simplest expression of the message we want to communicate. This is not the theme or slogan; the words of the proposition may never appear in advertising; yet all advertising must communicate the thought of the proposition.

The proposition for the Nixon for President primary advertising can be stated like this:

There's an uneasiness in the land. A feeling that things aren't right. That we're moving in the wrong direction. That none of the solutions to our problems are working. That we're not being told the truth about what's going on.

The trouble is in Washington. Fix that and we're on our way to fixing everything. Step one: move LBJ out, move a Republican president in.

And of all the Republicans, the most qualified for the job by far is Richard M. Nixon. *More than any other Republican candidate for the Presidency, Richard Nixon will know what has to be done—and he'll know the best way to get it done.* We'll all feel a whole lot better knowing he's there in Washington running things instead of somebody else.

A proposition has to be supported in the advertising by facts. What are our facts? What does Richard Nixon have that makes him "the most qualified by far"?

Experience. On the national scene. In foreign affairs. He knows how the Federal government works, and how to make it work for the people. He's got it all over the other candidates in this respect.

Knowledgeability. Resulting from his experience. His travels. His conversations with the world's thinkers and achievers. His years of intensive study.

Intellectual ability. Formidable. A disciplined mind. Able to cope with the big problems, come up with new answers. Can more than hold his own in his dealings with other world leaders.

Acceptability. Where it counts. In the capitols of the world. In the top circles of business, politics, the professions. Not always loved, he is universally respected. Not glamorous, he does have a certain star quality going for him. Most doors are open to him.

Ability to form a top team. Running the country is not a one-man job. You have to have expert help—and Richard Nixon knows where the talent is. He can bring the best minds in the country into government, get them to working on our problems. He won't have to depend on home-town pals; he has ranged too far for too long to be thus hampered.

Toughness. A good man to have on your side. Won't be shoved around. Will stick to what he believes. Can he be brainwashed? Try.

Integrity. Although there were some doubts in the past, these have been dispelled by the years. Richard Nixon is now generally regarded as honest, a man who levels with people. (The way he is handled from now on should strengthen that impression —particularly important in light of the credibility issue.)

Conscientiousness. He is serious. Hardworking. Selfless. Thorough. When you've got Nixon on a problem, you've got the best of Nixon.

Vigorous. He is young, healthy, energetic—not really a big advantage over the other Republican candidates, who are equally vigorous, but still a fact.

Party unifier. Self-explanatory. Probably not of much use in advertising.

There are also negatives—but these don't have to be as damaging as some pessimists fear. If we recognize them, deal with them intelligently instead of worrying about them, their effect can be minimized. What, then, does Richard Nixon lack?

Newness. Which is not a total negative. Newness means excitement—but it also means inexperience. And we don't have time for on-the-job training. When the chips are down, not too important.

Glamour. True. But again, when the chips are down, etc.

Humor. Can be corrected to a degree, but let's not be too obvious about it. Romney's cornball attempts have hurt him. If we're going to be witty, let a pro write the words.

Warmth. He can be helped greatly in this respect by how he is handled, by what he says and how he says it, etc. Will be discussed in more detail later.

There are other negatives which are supposed to be working against Mr. Nixon but—in this writer's opinion—they now seem to be part of a past that few people remember or much care about today. In this category we can place the "tricky Dick" image, the reputation for meanness and ruthlessness, for putting politics ahead of principle, etc. These now seem strangely out-of-date and no longer applicable to the man who is running in 1968.

A negative that does seem to hang on, however, is the loser image. This is a negative of special significance in the primaries; people don't want to waste their vote on a candidate who can't win the national election. Of course, there's nothing like winning to bury a reputation for losing. That's why Nixon's electability—

as shown in the polls, by what people are saying, in the first primaries, etc.—should be an important element of our advertising content. More on this later.

The foregoing has been a discussion of *what* we want to communicate—or, in the case of the negatives, what we may want to counteract. It can all be summed up in the next to last sentence of the proposition:

> *More than any other Republican candidate for the Presidency*, Richard Nixon will know *what* has to be done—and he'll know *the best way* to *get* it done.

It is imperative that this thought come through loud and clear in every single piece of advertising. If it doesn't, the advertising is not doing its job.

The execution, or the "how," of the advertising

In developing actual advertisements and commercials, we should observe two general guidelines.

First, the style of the advertising must be *appropriate*—to the man, to his background, to the office he is seeking. We are representing in our advertising a former vice president of the United States, a man with specific and well known personality traits, a candidate for the most important office in the world.

Cuteness, obliqueness, wayoutness, slickness—any obvious gimmicks that say "Madison Ave. at work here"—should be avoided. They could, indeed, result in a public backlash that would hurt our candidate. Imaginative approaches, contemporary techniques —yes. But we must beware of "overcreativity," and make sure that the basic seriousness of our purpose shows plainly in everything we do.

Second, we must not, in our zeal (or in our preoccupation with the loser image), forget that *our candidate is the favorite*.

In every race we're entering, the polls show Richard Nixon well out in front—and pulling farther ahead every week. We do not, therefore, have to take the kind of chances which a lesser known or less popular candidate might be tempted to take. We can afford a "careful confidence." (It's to be hoped that this would be reflected in Mr. Nixon's public appearances as well as in the advertising; there are times when his seriousness, and his determination to make a point, start coming across as defensive or even a little desperate. More cool is called for.)

At this point these notes will digress somewhat to analyze the forces behind the Nixon Resurgence (which are not too different from the forces which are moving Rockefeller to the fore) and comment on the "new Nixon" myth.

It's interesting to note that Mr. Nixon's growing popularity is not resulting from anything new he is saying or doing. What is happening is a political process of elimination on a mass scale, coupled with the cumulative effects of the "prior approval" factor. Listen to this dialogue with last year's typical Republican voter:

"We're in a mess," says the voter. "Gotta get LBJ out. Gotta get our boy in."
"You mean Nixon?"
"No, no. We've *been* there."
"Who, then?"
"I don't know. Ask me next year."

Time passes. Here we are in an election year. Can't cop out any more. Have to face up.

"Okay, Mr. Republican voter, so if you don't like Nixon, who *do* you want?"

"Well, there's Romney—old Super Square—he looked pretty good until he started talking. Reagan—a glamour boy and better than I expected but he still has to prove he could handle the Top Job. Percy—attractive but I really don't know much about him. Rockefeller—yeah, I could go with him, except he keeps saying he doesn't want to be President. That leaves Nixon."

"But you said you didn't like him."

"Yeah. But I can't seem to remember why. There's no deny-ing he's qualified. In fact, he's really a good man for the job. And I've been reading some very favorable things about him. And I've heard a lot of savvy people are getting behind him. Nixon? Sure—he'd get my vote!"

The point of all this is simply that it's not a "new Nixon" that's now at the top of the polls. It's the old Nixon with his strengths looking stronger and his negatives blurred by the years—and, if he's not quite the White Knight we saw in our dreams, he's still the best man by far we could send to Washington. And remember all those new voters for whom there can't be a new Nixon because they never knew the original Nixon: for them there's only Nixon '68—and compared to the others (with the possible exception of Reagan) that ain't bad!

In short, it's the attitude of the voters that's new—not Mr. Nixon. The advertising, therefore, should not strain to create a brand new image—because the old one's doing pretty well. Add a little warmth, a touch of humor, an aura of confidence—then publicize poll results, favorable articles, friendly quotes, and any-thing else that says, "winner"—and we can stay in front to the end.

Summing up the creative guidelines:

—Make sure the advertising is *appropriate*.
—Remember that *we are ahead*.
—Forget the "new Nixon" nonsense. It's the *new voter atti-tude* that's important.

Now let's look at a few specific ways we can accomplish our objectives:

Endorsements. No advertising will ever have the influence that a friend's opinion has. Fifty million dollars worth of Ford adver-tising can't convince you like your neighbor's comment, "Best car I ever owned." This is the "prior approval" factor at work; *he* likes it, so maybe *I* would (or should) too. It's a factor that seems to be working now for Richard Nixon—and one we should exploit.

Think back to our typical Republican voter as he mentally eliminates the other candidates one by one. He *wants* to be for Nixon; all he needs is the kind of nudge he'd get from hearing that a lot of people he respects are also for Nixon. He needs assurance that his opinion will have acceptance, that he won't look like a loner, or a nut. Or, if he is still plagued by the old Nixon negatives, the fact that knowledgeable people all around him are swinging to Nixon could prompt him to say to himself, "Maybe I better reexamine my thinking. If all those people are for him, there's a chance I could be wrong . . ." etc. An endorsement is also an effective way of talking about the candidate in the third person; the endorser can say things quite naturally about the candidate that the candidate could not comfortably say about himself.

Of course, an endorsement could have a negative effect on a voter who doesn't like the endorser; this possibility can be minimized by always presenting more than one endorser (a series of six or seven or eight short endorsements in a TV commercial, for instance). This has the extra advantage of emphasizing the unifying and acceptability aspects of Richard Nixon—as well as creating a bandwagon impression.

Polls. These are really tabulated endorsements, and can have the same kind of "prior approval" effect described above. They can, moreover, be used to promote the idea that Richard Nixon can win nationally. As we said earlier, the best way to bury a reputation for losing is to start winning. Advertising favorable out-of-state poll results in New Hampshire (where the wasted vote is a real concern) might convince voters that when they vote for Richard Nixon they're backing a man who can go all the way.

About RN on TV. There's a school of thought that says keep him off the tube, it's not his medium, etc. In this writer's opinion, that's giving up too easily. We know we're going to use television; it's our most powerful medium. But to use it for a series of commercials which do not show the candidate, as has been suggested, would inevitably arouse suspicion. What're we hiding? So let's decide now that Mr. Nixon *will* appear in our paid television announcements and start figuring out the best ways to present him. A few thoughts:

The more informally he is presented the better.

He looks good in motion.

He should be presented in some kind of "situation" rather than cold in a studio. The situation should look unstaged, even if it's not. A newsreel-type on location interview technique, for example, could be effective. The more visually interesting and local the location the better.

Avoid closeups. A medium waist shot is about as tight as the camera should get. He looks good when he faces the camera head-on.

Still photographs can be effectively used on TV. Interesting cropping, artful editing and juxtaposition of scenes, an arresting sound track, can all combine to make an unusual presentation. Added advantages: there's a wide range of material to choose from, and we'd be free to select only the most flattering pictures.

For short programs (a series of nightly 5-minute shows during the final two weeks is being proposed for New Hampshire) a "town meeting" format should be considered. Each one could take place in a different local meeting place—school, store, fire house, home, etc.) A group of thirty or forty people would be invited. The program could open with an exterior establishing shot, show Mr. Nixon entering, applause, then a few brief comments, a question and answer period, and closing remarks. A voice over announcer could handle the opening and sign off.

The matter of Mr. Nixon projecting more "warmth" and "humanness" has been discussed at great length. (This applies to all of his public appearances as well as the advertising.) Presenting him informally as suggested above will help. Another suggestion: give him words to say that will show his *emotional* involvement in the issues. He is inclined to be too objective, too much the lawyer building a case, too cold and logical. Buchanan wrote about RFK talking about the starving children in Recife. *That's* what we have to inject—because all of our problems, from Viet Nam to the cities to race to inflation are all *people* problems. A casualty is not a statistic, it's an American boy dying. Inflation is not percentage points, it's the price of bacon. Mr. Nixon recognizes this, of course, but he should make more of a point of displaying his feelings, as well as his knowledge. It would also help if his choice of words and phrases was more colorful. He should be more quotable, use interesting and unusual labels, dynamic references—occasionally new similes or metaphors.

Extracts from *Understanding Media*

Distributed among the Richard Nixon staff

MARSHALL McLUHAN

On the Jack Paar show for March 8, 1963, Richard Nixon was Paared down and remade into a suitable TV image. It turns out that Mr. Nixon is both a pianist and a composer. With sure tact for the character of the TV medium, Jack Paar brought out this "pianoforte" side of Mr. Nixon with excellent effect. Instead of the slick, glib, legal Nixon, we saw the doggedly creative and modest performer. A few timely touches like this would have quite altered the result of the Kennedy-Nixon campaign. TV is a medium that rejects the sharp personality and favors the presentation of processes rather than of products.

[p. 269]

An article on Perry Como bills him as "Low-pressure king of a high-pressure realm." The success of any TV performer depends on his achieving a low-pressure style of presentation, although getting his act on the air may require much high-pressure organization. Castro may be a case in point. According to Tad Szulc's story on "Cuban Television's One-man Show" ("The Eighth Art"), "in his seemingly improvised 'as-I-go-along' style he can evolve politics and govern his country—right on camera." Now, Tad Szulc is under the illusion that TV is a hot medium, and suggests that in the Congo "television might have helped Lumumba to incite the masses to even greater turmoil and bloodshed." But he is quite wrong. Radio is the medium for frenzy, and it has been the major means of hotting up the tribal blood of Africa, India, and China alike. TV has cooled Cuba down, as it is cooling down America. What the Cubans are getting by TV is the experience of being directly engaged in the making of political decisions. Castro presents himself as a teacher, and as Szulc says, "manages to blend political guidance and education with propaganda so skillfully that it is often difficult to tell where one begins and the other ends." Exactly the same mix is used in entertainment in Europe and America alike.

[pp. 270–71]

In a group of simulcasts of several media done in Toronto a few years back, TV did a strange flip. Four randomized groups of university students were given the same information. One group received it via radio, one from TV, one by lecture, and one read it. For all but the reader group, the information was passed along in straight verbal flow by the same speaker without discussion or questions or use of blackboard. Each group had half an hour of exposure to the material. Each was asked to fill in the same quiz afterward. It was quite a surprise to the experimenters when the students performed better with TV-channeled information and with radio than they did with lecture and print—and the TV group stood *well* above the radio group. Since nothing had been done to give special stress to any of these four media, the experiment was repeated with other randomized groups. This time each medium was allowed full opportunity to do its stuff. For radio and TV, the material was dramatized with many auditory and visual features. The lecturer took full advantage of the blackboard and class discussion. The printed form was embellished with an imaginative use of typography and page layout to stress each point in the lecture. All of these media had been stepped up to high intensity for this repeat of the original performance. Television and radio once again showed results high above lecture and print. Unexpectedly to the testers, however, radio now stood significantly above television. It was a long time before the obvious reason declared itself, namely that TV is a cool, participant medium. When hotted up by dramatization and stingers, it performs less well because there is less opportunity for participation. Radio is a hot medium. When given additional intensity, it performs better. It doesn't invite the same degree of participation in its users. Radio will serve as background-sound or as noise-level control, as when the ingenious teenager employs it as a means of privacy. TV will not work as background. It engages you. You have to be *with* it. (The phrase has gained acceptance since TV.)

[p. 271]

As in any other mosaic, the third dimension is alien to TV, but it can be superimposed. In TV the illusion of the third dimension is provided slightly by the stage sets in the studio; but the TV image itself is a flat two-dimensional mosaic. Most of the three-dimensional illusion is a carry-over of habitual viewing of film and photo. For the TV camera does not have a built-in angle of vision like the movie camera. Eastman Kodak now has a two-dimensional camera that can match the flat effects of the TV camera. Yet it is hard for illiterate people, with their habit of fixed points of view and three-dimensional vision, to understand the properties of two-dimensional vision. If it had been easy for them, they would have had no difficulties with abstract art, General Motors would not have made a mess of motorcar design, and the picture magazine would not be having difficulties now with the relationship between features and ads. The TV image requires each instant that we "close" the spaces in the mesh by a convulsive sensuous participation that is profoundly kinetic and tactile, because tactility is the interplay of the senses, rather than the isolated contact of skin and object.

To contrast it with the film shot, many directors refer to the TV image as one of "low definition," in the sense that it offers little detail and a low degree of information, much like the cartoon. A TV close-up provides only as much information as a small section of a long-shot on the movie screen.

[p. 273]

The TV image is of low intensity or definition, and therefore, unlike film, it does not afford detailed information about objects. The difference is akin to that between the old manuscripts and the printed word. Print gave intensity and uniform precision, where before there had been a diffuse texture. Print brought in the taste for exact measurement and repeatability that we now associate with science and mathematics.

The TV producer will point out that speech on television must not have the careful precision necessary in the theater. The TV actor does not have to project either his voice or himself. Likewise, TV acting is so extremely intimate, because of the peculiar involvement of the viewer with the completion or "closing" of the TV image, that the actor must achieve a great degree of spontaneous casualness that would be irrelevant in movies and lost on stage. For the audience participates in the inner life of the TV actor as fully as in the outer life of the movie star. Technically, TV tends to be a close-up medium. The close-up that in the movie is used for shock is, on TV, a quite casual thing. And whereas a glossy photo the size of the TV screen would show a dozen faces in adequate detail, a dozen faces on the TV screen are only a blur.

[p. 276]

A cool medium, whether the spoken word or the manuscript or TV, leaves much more for the listener or user to do than a hot medium. If the medium is of high definition, participation is low. If the medium is of low intensity, the participation is high. Perhaps this is why lovers mumble so.

Because the low definition of TV insures a high degree of audience involvement, the most effective programs are those that present situations which consist of some process to be completed. Thus, to use TV to teach poetry would permit the teacher to concentrate on the poetic process of actual *making*, as it pertained to a particular poem. The book form is quite unsuited to this type of involved presentation. The same salience of process to do-it-yourself-ness and depth involvement in the TV image extends to the art of the TV actor. Under TV conditions, he must be alert to improvise and to embellish every phrase and verbal resonance with details of gesture and posture, sustaining that intimacy with the viewer which is not possible on the massive movie screen or on the stage.

[p. 278]

With TV came the end of bloc voting in politics, a form of specialism and fragmentation that won't work since TV. Instead of the voting bloc, we have the icon, the inclusive image. Instead of a political viewpoint or platform, the inclusive political posture or stance. Instead of the product, the process. In periods of new and rapid growth there is a blurring of outlines. In the TV image we have the supremacy of the blurred outline, itself the maximal incentive to growth and new "closure" or completion. . . .

[p. 280]

It is an especially touchy area that presents itself with the question: "What has been the effect of TV on our political life?" Here, at least, great traditions of critical awareness and vigilance testify to the safeguards we have posted against the dastardly uses of power.

When Theodore White's *The Making of the President: 1960* is opened at the section on "The Television Debates," the TV student will experience dismay. White offers statistics on the number of sets in American homes and the number of hours of daily use of these sets, but not one clue as to the nature of the TV image or its effects on candidates or viewers. White considers the "content" of the debates and the deportment of the debaters, but it never occurs to him to ask why TV would inevitably be a disaster for a sharp intense image like Nixon's and a boon for the blurry, shaggy texture of Kennedy.

At the end of the debates, Philip Deane of the London *Observer* explained my idea of the coming TV impact on the election to the *Toronto Globe and Mail* under the headline of "The Sheriff and the Lawyer," October 15, 1960. It was that TV would prove so entirely in Kennedy's favor that he would win the election. Without TV, Nixon had it made. Deane, toward the end of his article, wrote:

"Now the press has tended to say that Mr. Nixon has been gaining in the last two debates and that he was bad in the first. Professor McLuhan thinks that Mr. Nixon has been sounding progressively more definite; regardless of the value of the Vice President's views and principles, he has been defending them with too much flourish for the TV medium. Mr. Kennedy's rather sharp responses have been a mistake, but he still presents an image closer to the TV hero, Professor McLuhan says—something like the shy young Sheriff—while Mr. Nixon with his very dark eyes that tend to stare, with his slicker circumlocution, has resembled more the railway lawyer who signs leases that are not in the interests of the folks in the little town.

"In fact, by counterattacking and by claiming for himself, as he does in the TV debates, the same goals as the Democrats have, Mr. Nixon may be helping his opponent by blurring the Kennedy image, by confusing what exactly it is that Mr. Kennedy wants to change.

"Mr. Kennedy is thus not handicapped by clear-cut issues; he is visually a less-well-defined image, and appears more nonchalant. He seems less anxious to sell himself than does Mr. Nixon. So far, then, Professor McLuhan gives Mr. Kennedy the lead without underestimating Mr. Nixon's formidable appeal to the vast conservative forces of the United States."

[pp. 287–88]

Analysis

BY WILLIAM GAVIN, OF THE RICHARD NIXON
STAFF

mcluhan etc:

so what does all this mean in practical political terms? for one thing, we're talking at the same time to two quite differently conditioned generations: the visual, linear older generation, and the aural, tactile, suffusing younger generation.

the bobby phenomenon; his screaming appeal to the tv generation. this certainly has nothing to do with logical persuasion; it's a total *experience*, a tactile sense—thousands of little girls who want him to be president so they can have him on the tv screen and run their fingers through the image of his hair. those who are aural-tactile conditioned are much more emotional, more tribal; information doesn't arrange itself in compartmented, linear, logical patterns, it's a collection, an assemblage, of random impressions, not necessarily connected except by the coincidence of their coexistence. a coexistent world.

we leave spaces for them to fill in in their own minds, like filling in the cartoon; low-definition, like bobby's rhetoric, which conveys an emotional posture without bothering with a reasoned analysis. it's the emotion that gets across, the posture, the sense of involvement and concern. lbj can never achieve this; he doesn't project, or if he does it's with a calculated intensity. it's got to appear non-calculated, incomplete—*incomplete,* that's it, the circle never squared, the random gobs of attitude.

must be mutual frustration—the young frustrated by the linear rationality of the over-30-dominated culture, and the old frustrated by the aural irrationality of the under-30s. "never trust anyone over (under) 30" takes on a new meaning when seen this way, and even a measure of validity. we're talking about groups that have been conditioned by two different worlds, the pre-tv and the post-tv environments.

one thing it all means is that we should have two separate sets of materials, one for the visual and one for the aural; there's probably no great harm in one group's seeing the stuff meant for the other, but each should see the stuff meant for itself.

reagan manages to appeal to both at the same time; he's the tv candidate, who instinctively reaches the aural-tactile; he speaks with a linear logic, and his quick simplicisms appeal to children old and young.

dirksen is camp.

to the tv-oriented, it's doubly important that we make them *like* the candidate. they're emotional, unstructured, uncompartmented, direct; there's got to be a straight communication that doesn't get wound through the linear translations of logic.

rule 1: what you don't say can be more important than what you do say. what you leave unsaid then becomes what the audience brings to it—lead 'em to the brink of the idea, but don't push across the brink. it's not the words, but the silences, where the votes lie.

new hampshire: saturation with a film, in which candidate can be shown better than he can be shown in person because it can be edited, so only the best moments are shown; then a quick parading of the candidate in the flesh so that the guy they've gotten intimately acquainted with on the screen takes on a living presence—not saying anything, just being seen, so there's the physical presence, the eye-contact.

with the film, they get to know him as a person, not as a headline; and in color, not in grainy black-and-white of a newspaper picture.

all this especially pertinent, maybe even to older generation, at a time when people not intensively concentrating on politics. reason requires a high degree of discipline, of concentration; impression is easier.

reason pushes the viewer back, it assaults him, it demands that he agree or disagree; impression can envelop him, invite him in, without making an intellectual demand, or a demand on his intellectual energies. he can receive the impression without having to think about it in a linear, structured way. when we argue with him we demand that he make the effort of replying. we seek to engage his intellect, and for most people this is the most difficult work of all. the emotions are more easily roused, closer to the surface, more malleable.

get the voters to like the guy, and the battle's two thirds won.

on the other hand, maybe some of the intense distrust of bobby stems from the unarticulated suspicion that this is just what he's up to: conning the public by means of an image saturation, without any logical substance behind it. the nation's problems demand logical analysis and logical treatment; and yet a lot of people, especially the young, react against logic, and maybe one of the sources of bobby's appeal to the young is, at the same time, just this: that he's not logical, he holds out the promise, implied though not explicit, that things can be solved without logic, but just with "love," etc.

Memorandum

RAY PRICE

28 November 1967

FROM: Ray Price
SUBJ: Recommendations for General Strategy from Now through
Wisconsin

We enter with these factors in the equation:

1) RN is the front-runner, maintaining or increasing strength
in the polls with relatively little activity.

2) We can't be sure how solid this support is (e.g., the New
Hampshire attitude that he's a good man but probably can't win,
thus their votes are really being cast away—or cast for LBJ).

3) Romney is certain to conduct a high-intensity campaign,
with a lot of street-cornering and probably a lot of TV. This has
apparently been effective in Michigan; whether it's transferable
to a 1968 Presidential campaign is another question.

4) Rockefeller and Reagan continue to exercise their attrac-
tions from the sidelines. *Rockefeller's strength derives principally
from RN's can't-win image.* He's riding high, not particularly because people like him, but because they've been told (which is
something other than thinking) that he can win and that he thus
is the only realistic alternative to LBJ. At this stage of the game,
poll results don't particularly show what voters think about a
candidate; they reflect in large measure what they've been told.
They haven't begun thinking that intensively. Reagan's strength
derives from personal charisma, glamor, but primarily the ideological fervor of the Right and the emotional distress of those who
fear or resent the Negro, and who expect Reagan somehow to
keep him "in his place"—or at least to echo their own anger and
frustration.

RN is the overwhelming favorite of the delegate types; if we can lick the can't-win thing we've got it made. *This is the one possible obstacle between RN and the nomination.* Thus the whole thrust of our effort should be aimed at erasing this image.

How?

To answer this, we have to analyse the image.

Basically, it divides into two parts:

    a) He lost his last two elections.

    b) He somehow "feels" like a loser.

We can't alter the facts of (a), and probably our capacity to get people to look at those facts realistically is limited. We can make any number of powerful arguments about the way in which those results should be interpreted: in 1960, one of the closest races in history against one of the most charismatic of American political figures, the effect of the Catholic issue, vote-stealing, defending the Eisenhower record, etc.; and in 1962, the bitter split in the California Republican party, the fact that he wasn't credible as a mere governor (too big for the job, and he showed it), etc. But politics is only minimally a rational science, and no matter how compelling these arguments—even if we can get people to sit down and listen to them—they'll only be effective *if* we can get the people to make the *emotional* leap, or what theologians call "the leap of faith." If we can make them *feel* that he's got the aura of a winner, they'll rationalize away the past defeats by themselves; if we can't make them feel that, no matter what the rational explanations, they'll pull down the mental blind marked with those simple words, "he lost."

The natural human use of reason is to support prejudices, not to arrive at opinions.

Then how do we attack (b)—the notion that he "feels" like a loser?

First, we bear in mind that to a lot of people he feels like a winner. It's the others we have to worry about. And we might oversimplify by dividing these into two basic groups: 1) those who *themselves* feel there's "something about him I don't like," or "something about him that spells loser"; and 2) those who themselves react altogether positively, but consider him a loser-type because of the way *others* react to him. The line between these two groups, of course, isn't sharp; and again we have to bear in mind that most people's reactions to most public figures are a mixture of positives and negatives. But for purposes of analysis, we can proceed from this division.

Polls showing RN substantially ahead can be of considerable use, particularly with those of Group (2). But there's a caveat here: poll strength is bound to fluctuate, and to the extent that our defenses against "can't-win" are built on polls, they're insecure. A slight downturn then could have a snowball effect. But if we can erase the *feeling* of "can't-win," then we can survive a substantial buffeting by the polls.

The hard core of the problem lies with those who themselves feel there's "loser" somehow written on him—i.e., with Group (1). If we can get these, we'll automatically get Group (2).

Again, we might divide the factors entering into the "can't-win" feeling into two broad categories: (a) historical, and (b) personal. The historical factors would, of course, include the fact of the two losses, but they run deeper. In a sense, they're all wrapped up in the fact that for years Nixon was one of those men it was fashionable to hate. It might take people a moment to remember *why* they were supposed to hate him, but they do remember that they were. Even in communities where he was locally popular, it was well known that he was hated elsewhere— and particularly in many of the Best Circles.

Generally, the sources of this hate centered around the way he practiced, or was alleged to practice, his political craft. Whatever the strange complex of passions that went into the hysterical anti-anti-communism of the postwar and McCarthy years; whatever the emotional responses of those who disliked his style, the essence of the objections lay in Nixon's cutting edge. He was viewed as a partisan figure first, a national figure second; as devious and unfair in his debating tactics—a master of unsupported innuendo, etc.

Let's leave realities aside—because what we have to deal with now is not the facts of history, but an image of history. The history we have to be concerned with is not what happened, but what's remembered, which may be quite different. Or, to put it another way, the historical untruth may be a political reality.

We can't do anything about what *did* happen, and there's not much we can *directly* do about people's *impressions* of what happened; for better or for worse, these are part of the political folklore. Thus what we have to do is to persuade people that they're irrelevant to 1968. How? This has three prongs:

1. The passage of time; this has clearly worked in our favor. The sharp edge of memory has dulled, the image has mellowed; people don't maintain their passions forever. Also, Stewart Alsop makes an interesting point in his 1960 book, "Nixon and Rockefeller": that with a couple of minor exceptions, "after 1954 the anti-Nixon dossier dwindles away into almost nothing at all. . . . The fact is that, since 1954, Nixon has very rarely gone too far, although the provocation has often been great." (pp. 152–53)

2. A dawning recognition on the part of some voters that they (or the chroniclers) might have been wrong, and that maybe the horror stories weren't all true after all; and

3. The natural phenomenon of growth. This is where I think there's the most gold to be mined. People understand growth, readily and instinctively; they expect people to mellow as they mature, and to learn from experience. Particularly in the case of a person with RN's recognized ability and intelligence, they'd be surprised if he didn't grow and change with the years. This doesn't mean a "new Nixon"; it simply means the natural maturation of the same Nixon, and in this context it makes the leaving behind of the old stereotypes perfectly acceptable and understandable. *The great advantage of the growth idea is that it doesn't require a former Nixon-hater to admit that he was wrong in order to become a Nixon supporter now;* he can still cherish his prejudices of the past, he can still maintain his own sense of infallibility, even while he shifts his position on a Nixon candidacy.

But what of the personal factors, as opposed to the historical?

These tend to be more a gut reaction, unarticulated, non-analytical, a product of the particular chemistry between the voter and the *image* of the candidate. *We have to be very clear on this point: that the response is to the image, not to the man,* since 99 percent of the voters have no contact with the man. It's not what's *there* that counts, it's what's projected—and, carrying it one step further, it's not what *he* projects but rather what the voter receives. It's not the man we have to change, but rather the *received impression*. And this impression often depends more on the medium and its use than it does on the candidate himself.

Politics is much more emotional than it is rational, and this is particularly true of Presidential politics. People identify with a President in a way they do with no other public figure. Potential presidents are measured against an ideal that's a combination of leading man, God, father, hero, pope, king, with maybe just a touch of the avenging Furies thrown in. They want him to be larger than life, a living legend, and yet quintessentially human; someone to be held up to their children as a model; someone to be cherished by themselves as a revered member of the family, in somewhat the same way in which peasant families pray to the icon in the corner. Reverence goes where power is; it's no coincidence that there's such persistent confusion between love and fear in the whole history of man's relationship to his gods. Awe enters into it.

And we shouldn't credit the press with a substantially greater leaven of reason than the general public brings. The press may be better at rationalizing their prejudices, but the basic response remains an emotional one.

Selection of a President has to be an act of faith. It becomes increasingly so as the business of government becomes ever more incomprehensible to the average voter. This faith isn't achieved by reason; it's achieved by charisma, by a *feeling* of trust that can't be argued or reasoned, but that comes across in those silences that surround the words. The words are important—but less for what they actually say than for the sense they convey, for the impression they give of the man himself, his hopes, his standards, his competence, his intelligence, his essential humanness, and the directions of history he represents.

Most countries divide the functions of head of government (prime minister) and chief of state (king or president). We don't. The traditional "issues" type debates center on the role of the head of government, but I'm convinced that people vote more for a chief of state—and this is primarily an emotional identification, embracing both a man himself and a particular vision of the nation's ideals and its destiny.

All this is a roundabout way of getting at the point that we should be concentrating on building a *received* image of RN as the kind of man proud parents would ideally want their sons to grow up to be: a man who embodies the national ideal, its aspirations, its dreams, a man whose *image* the people want in their homes as a source of inspiration, and whose voice they want as the representative of their nation in the councils of the world, and of their generation in the pages of history.

That's what being a "winner" means, in Presidential terms.

What, then, does this mean in terms of our uses of time and of media between now and April 2?

For one thing, it means investing whatever time RN needs in order to work out firmly in his own mind that vision of the nation's future that he wants to be identified with. This is crucial. It goes beyond the choice of a slogan, beyond the choice of a few key "issues"; it's essential to the projection of RN as the man for the '70s.

Secondly, it suggests that we take the time and the money to experiment, in a controlled manner, with film and television techniques, with particular emphasis on pinpointing those *controlled* uses of the television medium that can *best* convey the *image* we want to get across.

I know the whole business of contrived image-mongering is repugnant to RN, with its implication of slick gimmicks and phony merchandising. But it's simply not true that honesty is its own salesman; for example, it takes make-up to make a man look natural on TV. Similarly, it takes art to convey the truth from us to the viewer. And we have to bear constantly in mind that it's not what we say that counts, but what the listener hears; not what we project, but how the viewer receives the impression. I think it was Luce and Hadden, in their original prospectus for *Time,* who laid down the rule that it's not what the editors put into a magazine that counts, but what the readers get out of it—and that rule is just as applicable to us.

The TV medium itself introduces an element of distortion, in terms both of its effect on the candidate and of the often subliminal ways in which the image is received. And it inevitably is going to convey a partial image—thus ours is the task of finding how to control its use so the part that gets across is the part we want to have gotten across.

Our concentrated viewing of clips from the CBS library left a clear impression that RN comes across decidedly unevenly— sometimes rather badly, sometimes exceedingly well, and that the greater the element of informality and spontaneity the better he comes across. This spontaneity is difficult to get in the formal setting of a standard press conference or a set speech, when he's concentrating on the arrangement of words to convey a particular thought in a particular way. Apart from all the technical gimmicks, the key difference in LBJ's TV manner at his last press conference—and what really brought it off so stunningly—was that he was no longer trying to formulate sentences in a precise and guarded manner; he gave the impression of being no longer self-conscious about his *manner* of expression, but rather seemed to have his mind fixed on the thing he was talking *about*. It was this apparent unselfconsciousness that unleashed the power of the man; and this unselfconsciousness is the essence of spontaneity. Suddenly, LBJ was transformed from a man with a can't-win television image to a man with a can-win image, and the lesson ought not to be lost on us.

We have to capture and capsule this spontaneity—and this means shooting RN in situations in which it's likely to emerge, then having a chance to edit the film so that the parts shown are the parts we want shown. We need to build a library of such shots, which then will be available for a variety of uses—and so that, in minimum time, we can put together a variety of one- or five-minute or longer *films of the man in motion,* with the idea of conveying a sense of his *personality*—the personality that most voters have simply not had a chance to see, or, if they have, have lost in the montage of other images that form their total perceptions of the man.

The Paul Niven show came across brilliantly, and it was a fine example of an appearance in which the circumstances were right: a relaxed, informal setting; a "conversation" rather than a Meet-the-Press-type adversary proceeding; sufficient time and scope to expand on the ideas presented; a chance to bring out the qualities of the man. The people who say Nixon "can't win" tend to have a two-dimensional, black-and-white image of him; *this kind of show makes it possible to bring out a third dimension,* and it's in this third dimension that the keys to victory lie.

In this third dimension, style and substance are inseparable. And the substantive essence is not whatever facts may be adduced (though facts are valuable), but the sense of attitudes and approaches which have been *thought through,* not only in depth, but also in terms of their relationship to those other processes of government and aspects of society that they may affect.

One of our great assets for 1968 is the sense that RN comes to the fray freshened by an experience rare among men in public life, and unique among those of his generation: after a meteoric rise, followed by eight years at the center of power and the grinding experience of a Presidential campaign, time as a private citizen to reflect on the lessons of public service, on the uses of power, on the directions of change—*and in so doing to develop a perspective on the Presidency that no serious candidate in this century has had the chance to achieve.* It's a perspective that an incumbent cannot have, because one has to get away from the office to see it whole; and that an outsider cannot have, because one has to have been there to know its nature.

Another thing we've got to get across is a sense of human warmth. This is vital to the Presidential mystique, and has largely been the "hidden side" of RN, as far as the public is concerned. And it can be gotten across without loss of either dignity or privacy. It shines through in a lot of those spontaneous moments that have been caught on film. It would be helped by an occasional groping for an answer. Just letting the girls be seen can be a big plus. It came through at times on the Niven show, and strongly on the Carson show. One of the great plusses of the Carson show was that it hit a lot of people with the *jolt of the unexpected*—it showed people a side of RN *that they didn't know existed, and this jarred loose a lot of the old prejudices and preconceptions.*

Getting across this sense of warmth does *not* require being a backslapper or a "buddy-buddy boy" or a hail-fellow-well-met. To attempt to be such would be not only transparently phony, but inappropriate; we're in a Presidential race, not at a Shriners' convention. It can and should be done subtly, naturally—and this is one of the great advantages of the TV medium (which is a close-up medium) in a relaxed setting, and also of film. Here the warmth *does* come across—in facial expressions, in the inflections of voice, in the thoughtful exposition of a problem *in human terms and in a low-key manner.*

Right now we should be concentrating as much as possible on "cool" uses of TV, and on "cool" impressions—both to establish likeability (it's in the cool use that the warmth comes through) and to fit the rhythms of a campaign that's going to hot up later. That is, we want to leave room on the upper end of the intensity scale, so that as we move toward November, we've got reaches of intensity—of "hotness"—to expand into.

So: we should use TV, but we should be selective in our uses of it. We don't need exposure for exposure's sake. We don't have to establish recognition. But we do want to close the gap between old myths and present realities: we want to remind supporters of the candidate's strengths, and demonstrate to non-supporters that the Herblock images are fiction. The way to do this is to let more people see the candidate as we see him, remembering that the important thing is not to win debates, but to win the audience; not to persuade them to RN's point of view, but to win their faith in his leadership.

Memorandum

LEN GARMENT

November 16, 1967

TO: RN
FROM: LG

Some key propositions relating to the thrust of the campaign have come into focus:

1. Basic Campaign Strategy.

I subscribe completely to Pat's fine memo as it relates to Nelson Rockefeller's strategy and the related problems of our approach to television. NR has a clearcut strategy that casts him above battle, invests him with an aura of statesmanship, and makes him increasingly attractive, because people believe he does not want the Presidency (they may be somewhat of two minds about this, but they are *inclined* to believe him and in any event, he is not involved in *saying* things that bother one group or another.) This strategy is working for NR because it is natural to his position as Governor—it is easy for him to stick to, because *he has no options*. Granted RN cannot approach the electorate with quite so monolithic a strategy; and granted that there are competing tactical arguments of much greater complexity—nevertheless, I think it imperative to devise and stay with a counterpart strategy which is on the same level. It must—to the extent possible—get RN above the battle, moving *away* from politics and *toward* statesmanship. It will have to be different from NR's in its details (because the situations are different), but the objective must be the same. *Like NR, RN must use strategic rather than tactical weap-*

ons insofar as his own personal effort is concerned. To put it in perhaps an oversimplified way, it seems to me this means a fundamentally philosophical orientation, consistently executed, rather than a program-oriented, issues-oriented, or "down-in-the-streets" campaign. The latter—which well-meaning friends no less than self-seeking local politicians, state chairman, etc., will strenuously urge—leads inevitably to the lowest common denominator of conventional "politics" and its concomitants: irritation or boredom of the general public; exposure to battering by uncontrolled local and national media; exhaustion; depletion by diffusion of campaign resources (men and money); lack of focus; reinforcing old stereotypes; problems with the polls; etc. Conversely, as the men inevitably thrust into the arena scar each other, the sideline operators will wax fat. The continuation of a routine tactical approach by RN is an intrinsic part of NR's strategy, and is the key to the massive attack on RN which the national media friendly to that strategy are geared to employ in the next and crucial stage of the pre-convention campaign. *Our approach must at least be thought through on a disciplined and critical basis with this hypothesis in mind.*

(It also occurs to me that it may be a good thing if some journalists begin to accept NR's disclaimers of interest in the Presidency as true (for whatever reason), so that the attention of voters in the primary states becomes focused increasingly on the actual choices.)

2. Issues, Programs or Philosophy.

The campaign should be set at the level of statecraft, rather than politics. This means a philosophical thrust, in which issues and program discussion is extremely selective and is used to *illustrate* points of philosophy, rather than as ends in themselves. The main areas are the functions of the modern-day President; the functions of government; how to marshal and coordinate the domestic resources of the nation (intellectual/technological/energy); and foreign policy in the next decade. In such a setting (which decisively focuses on the tasks of national leadership), there are many subjects to which RN is not required to address himself—certainly not in programmatic detail. Openness to ideas, familiarity with the levers of power in the political machinery, moral leadership, are the attitudes and themes to be developed.

It is not RN's business to have a "political" point of view toward everything under the sun (legalized abortion, drugs, hippies, miniskirts, jazz and so on). On many such subjects, he of course has a personal viewpoint (which may, or may not, go down with the majority), but this should be carefully set apart from his functions as a national leader. An effort to be all things to all men, or to have an "answer" to every question, tends toward a disastrous, boiled-down homogeneity—i.e., the stereotype of a politician. There is no harm at all in stating directly that RN doesn't know the details of this or that, provided a receptive attitude toward acquiring such information is displayed so that detailed knowledge can be developed where necessary. It strikes me that the prime function of national leadership in an incredibly complicated era is to coordinate the gathering of information by experts, to stimulate debate and discussion at all levels, to determine priorities, to guide legislation on matters which are in the national interest (and which may feasibly be articulated in legislation), to leave to the states, to municipalities, and to private persons and entities those activities best handled at such levels— *but in any event, to reserve the Presidential prestige and energy for matters of Presidential moment.*

This should be RN's central attitude, and clearly so, as he approaches not only the national campaign, *but the primaries as well.*

3. Research.

Closely related to the above discussion is the proposition that RN must be acquainted with issues, programs, ideas, etc., *but need not now be an originator of programs.* (Such an effort would be largely nonproductive or even harmful. People distrust most programs; don't comprehend the details; and are generally exasperated with the political motivation of most proposals.) Given RN's *existing* Presidential statute, his function is to approve this, reject that, point out what can work, what can't, and why. His interest is not in nuts and bolts, but with directions, potentials, and again, priorities. Realism as to what must be done, intelligent analysis as to why and how we should move, and confidence that what is necessary will be done, are the elements of the Presidential attitude. Governors and Congressmen can (and most do) offer programs—that is their *business*. RN must talk about *directions* for the next decade and beyond. What JFK referred to as the agenda of "unfinished national business" (second or third debate) should be RN's prime concern. Synthesizing the available raw material is the function of a statesman. Propounding the conventional political pieties and the details of this or that program is deadly, because it is dull, unconvincing and inevitably "political."

The mood to be conveyed by RN's words and writings and by *all* advertising and PR material (that is, with consistent thrust): Get the machinery of America functioning again. Harness the enormous latent energy of the people and summon up their sense of purpose—now buried in division and philosophical muddle. Recognize that the strength of America is in its *drive, intelligence, durability* and *experience*. It is a young but experienced nation. It is a mixture of seemingly conflicting qualities—ambitious, acquisitive, generous, practical, idealistic, pragmatic, restless— but all of these can be made to work together in the greatest machine for social as well as economic progress the world has ever known. These are the qualities of the nation. They must be rediscovered in new leadership in an era of renewal. These are RN's qualities buried under all the clichéd comments and questions about his stamina, persistence, perennial "newness"—i.e., "What makes Nixon run?" In short, *What makes America run?*

As to programs: Consciously or unconsciously, the voters *know* that the raw material is available. There are programs, ideas, data, experts. There is the fantastic economic machine. There are abundant national resources. What is needed is leadership that will shape the materials, get the creative machinery of American life working to move the nation forward. Sorting out the functions of government, *restoring a sense of unity,* is the national imperative. From a vast pool of talent—Governors, Senators, Congressmen, businessmen and intellectuals—the Republicans can draw the men, ideas and programs to staff the next government and administer its domestic and foreign concerns. Change, freshness, again a sense of where we want to go, *and most important, the capacity to organize and unify the country as well as the party,* must be communicated, not nuts and bolts, statistics, straddles, views on nonrelevant matters, funny hats, handshaking, small talk, and so on. What Bill Gavin describes as the "Nixon View" should come through with absolute clarity—the "view" itself being one that is clear, non-"political," not hackneyed.

In this connection, the only "program" idea I have heard that seems to me to have (a) the power to persuade, (b) emotional impact at many levels, (c) logical force—and can be made RN's own, because only he can make it seem a viable reality—is the Volunteer Army. I know there are political and fiscal problems. But I think it enough of a potential stroke to warrant the most serious consideration. I think everyone feels that the crises ahead require a professional army; and at the heart of much of the general anxiety about Vietnam (including much of the frenetic dissent) is the draft, for emotional rather than rational reasons. I think this extends to the mothers of three- and four-year olds, as well as the mothers of boys in their teens.

Other than this program, I think everything else is available on a pick, choose, pull together, and endorse basis (with one variation or another).

4. The NAM Speech.

This next major public occasion should be viewed as a command performance. Every effort should be made to use it to build our own "view" and work against the opposition strategy. *Prima facie,* the occasion is not a good one, for the obvious reason that it associates RN with the fat cat *status quo;* handled conventionally, it will produce a negative or neutral result. This may be all we can get under the circumstances, but the occasion does strike me as a *potential* plus if RN goes against the grain of the occasion. By this I do not mean that *preaching* to the businessmen would be any more productive than praising them. But I think they can be "summoned to the mountaintop" with a blunt, hard-hitting message on the social crisis which confronts all America, and the central responsibilities thereby cast on leaders of business and labor, as well as leaders of government at all levels. The ideological "polycentrism" of American politics (Moynihan's theme) is a relevant part, but only a part, of this message. (And here my contention is that there should be no attitude of smugness, i.e., "See what's happening to the liberals.") The obsolescence of "special interest" attitudes which go beyond competitiveness to the point of social destructiveness is a potential element (e.g., restrictive import legislation; inequitable tax privileges; racial and technological restrictions by big labor; problems of self-restraint on the part of unions whose memberships control vital public services). Another potential element is the weight to be given social profitability as opposed to dollar profitability in measuring corporate investment (i.e., do the same rate-of-return considerations apply to installation of water, air and noise pollution devices, job training programs, etc., as apply to traditional corporate activities?). Still another potential element: Isn't it time for the great inter-city companies, almost quasi-governmental in size and power, to begin to think of their contribution, without the carrot of special tax breaks, to the stability of the American social and economic structure? Certainly, American business knows that the alternative is the stick of greater federal intervention.

This is suggestive of the level at which I think this speech should be set. It should be bold, hortatory and utterly unexpected. Measured by what would most set NR's teeth on edge, I think a speech which was reported as surprisingly outspoken and a trenchant challenge to the *status quo* elements in big business, big labor and big government would be most effective. *From this standpoint,* the response (favorable or hostile) of the immediate audience would be largely irrelevant (although I'm inclined to think it is more likely to be favorable than hostile, if the speech goes to the jugular). *An apathetic response is the one thing to avoid.*

5. New Hampshire Research.

The early intimations from the group interviews indicate that foreign policy (Vietnam) is by far the major preoccupation among Republicans. The state may well be atypical; it seems that they are only remotely concerned about such things as riots, cities, the young people, even cost-of-living. They appear mainly concerned about the incomprehensible drift of foreign policy, the lack of comprehensible communication (or persuasion) about the war, the lack of defined goals ("In World War II, reaching Berlin was the end, in Korea, the 38th parallel, but in Vietnam, where, when?" etc.), the feeling that they were mousetrapped, the lack of credibility. The need for leadership dominates the talk so far.

Local issues seem to be mainly hospital facilities (chiefly for mental health) and educational facilities. They want a return to professional and believable government in Washington. RN's ability to unify the party in New Hampshire seems to be a very strong consideration. If the primary were held right now, it appears RN would win decisively. But the mood is one of anxiety, uncertainty, groping, etc. (McCarthy's entrance will undoubtedly complicate things, particularly if he turns out to be an eloquent critic of the war.)

6. Television, Advertising, Communications Generally.

The available elements are generally first-rate, but the operation as an entity is suffering badly from lack of coordination. As yet, there is no central approach, no clear-cut objective. *The organizations in primary states must be controlled and directed.* The Wisconsin agency—staffed with experienced, bright and highly motivated men—needs this as much as any other operation. The New York group (Treleaven, Shakespeare, Plesser, et al.) must furnish this; and now that they are beginning to see the direction of the preliminary work done in Wisconsin, their own work can go forward. All of us here (Ray, Pat, Bob E., Treleaven, Shakespeare) are agreed on certain basic problems. Solutions will depend in significant part on basic decisions as to the thrust of the campaign. As an example only, it may well be that an intensive and extremely specific creative effort in New York during December and January will furnish the basic program material and in a way that addresses itself to a group of problems—i.e., pressures for candidate availability, fund raising, adherence to a central theme, controlled material, etc. This *might* principally involve the use of film (largely existing footage plus some new shooting). The subject is too large to cover in this memo, but it represents the emerging thinking of a number of people close to

RN in relation to a variety of problems over-the-horizon. (Ray Price has a number of fresh and persuasive observations in this area.)

7. Staff.

Much progress will be achieved if the best available people are assembled and physically available to each other and to RN. Certain key people (Rose, Pat, Ray) are overwhelmed with paper/people/trivia, etc., in escalating (although presently unavoidable) proportions. They all need, and I think will get, help when organizational and facilities problems are overcome.

8. Recommendation.

RN should direct that a small group of his closest political advisors (Ellsworth, Buchanan, Price, Haldeman, Harlow, etc.) meet with the advertising and PR group (e.g., Treleaven, Shakespeare, Plesser, Winick) in the next two weeks and come up with an evaluation of the media/communications problem and propose a set of concrete recommendations. It would be most desirable if certain policy guidelines could be set in advance by RN, e.g., a definition of the general thrust of the campaign, a requirement that physical campaigning be held to a minimum, with certain stipulated exceptions to allow for political requirements and irreversible commitments.

NOTE: The foregoing is rough, fragmentary and designed to present a point of view, rather than a set of well-honed propositions.

Memorandum

WILLIAM GAVIN

competing with the new Johnson: We've got to establish a sense of a man in motion, of newness, freshness, vigor. LBJ is static, located, tied to the White House; he is *there*, in one place, in Washington, and however much he chases around the country he's still, conceptually, tied to the one location. The White House goes where he goes; conversely, wherever he goes he still is in the White House.

so this is opportunity #1. Motion. Which conveys a sense of vigor.

also need a sense of searching, which can tie in with the restless, searching, never-satisfied mood of today's young. To be self-satisfied is to be old; searching is a posture of youth. Youth moves.

LBJ's going to have more programs than we could begin to devise, so we don't want to compete with him on this. We've got to have the vision of the future that overleaps these; goals for the day after tomorrow, rather than programs for tomorrow. We're talking about the patterns of the '80s, because these are going to be set by the actions of the '70s.

dart around, nip at him from the sides, leap over him; don't go after him frontally. It's too strong a front.

this needs style: star style. LBJ's strong-man, big-man, tough-man, Colossus. Get warmth and wit and cool. Polish. A with-it candidate, who's not going to let this big tough guy run away with the country, who's going to move us forward, but sensibly, who's more reflective, less willful, who's responsive to the people, not just to the power sources; who's plugged in.

maybe we get at it through the idea that "people can be fun." An evidenced interest in persons, individuals, as individuals, in what makes 'em tick, in what they're like, in local idiosyncrasies

—a person-to-person communication that conveys a receptivity. Johnson overwhelms; maybe we should underwhelm. involve the viewer, the listener, draw him in, make him participate, convey the sense of welcome.

a guy who's self-contained and self-confident, but interested: "I'm what I am; what are you?"

a leader who's in touch with the world, and now is out to discover the *people* of America, even as he exposes his views and summons them to the new world. a give-and-take in which instead of getting caught in a debate over his views, he states 'em and then goes off on an exploration of his audience and its views. don't push; pull.

has to come across as a person larger than life, the stuff of legend. People are stirred by the legend, including the living legend, not by the man himself. It's the aura that surrounds the charismatic figure more than it is the figure itself, that draws the followers. Our task is to build that aura. *Attention begets attention.* People who wouldn't look twice at something happening in the street will if they see a crowd gathered to watch. People pant over movie stars in person not because they're inherently any more interesting than the person next door, but because they're a focus of public attention, of adulation. They're events, happenings, institutions, legends: see the legend in the flesh. it's something to tell the neighbors about.

Hold out ideals, things people aspire to, things people want to be identified with (even if they don't live by ideals, they like to think that they do).

Represent the best: the noblest.

Break away from linear logic: present a barrage of impressions. of attitudes. break off in mid-sentence and skip to something half a world away, that bears tangentially on what you've been talking about. wrap the subject around, envelop the audience in a kaleidoscope of impressions; this is three-dimensional. This may be the key: enveloping the audience, bringing it in, entwining it.

It's this three-dimensionality we've got to construct.

Color TV is far more three-dimensional than black-and-white. Black-and-white is, as McLuhan points out, a low-definition image, and the viewer tends to concentrate on a few main things and let his mind fill in the rest. In color, his eye picks out the other details. In black-and-white, the mind has to fill in the color, to translate from the black-and-white image to the world as our eye otherwise perceives it, i.e., in full color. Do we actually do this? I doubt it; I think that when watching black-and-white, we see a black-and-white world. Perhaps this concentrates attention more. Is there a contradiction here, between the concentrated attention and the mind's eye filling in details? Perhaps what it is is that the mind's eye fills them in, but not very fully, so that the memory is somewhat flatter than it is in color. Perhaps we remember the drama better in black-and-white, but the people come across more fully rounded in color. Especially if what we see is a relatively brief exposure, without much story-line. The story-line comes across more sharply in black and white, but the people we see in color are people as we see them in real life.

Camera techniques: at LBJ's press conference, when it swung around so that we saw the audience and the television equipment, etc., we were seeing the scene at least partly as LBJ saw it; thus, subliminally, we were with him; the camera made up partners, on the same team, looking through the same eyes. USE THIS! Get the camera to show what RN is seeing, bring the viewer into his viewpoint. so they identify. Walking: show what he's seeing as he's talking.

Johnson's new television personality makes this a whole new ball game.

So let's not be afraid of television gimmicks, but just ensure that those we use are in good taste and convey the right tone. His did. He was using the tools and techniques of television in order to conquer the medium, to use it to show the real LBJ rather than the pious hypocrite we've grown accustomed to. We've got to do the same.

We've got to do better.

We've got to capitalize on our strengths, to use whatever techniques can best project them.

Get across: quick, spontaneous, sparkle, a sense of excitement.

chief of state vs head of government, and the sense of a vacuum in the office of chief of state. LBJ not holding out the unfinished agenda. he's the guy you give the unfinished agenda to, with

209

instructions to make it happen. this was the great source of kennedy's appeal—the king bit. identify. jfk's ideal. clean, handsome, witty, articulate, rich, sure, pacesetter, stylesetter, elan, verve, guts, pushing ahead without being pushy.

we present the unfinished agenda, and suggest we'll hire people like lbj to achieve it.

above it all. a higher plane (planar politics, go into this)

doesn't matter if nothing gets done, as long as there's a sense of moving toward the higher ideals—with a bit of pork, i.e. ask not what your country, etc., while spelling out all the free goodies we're gonna offer; with this jfk managed to hold out the promise of a lot for nothing while at the same time absolving the recipients' consciences. the painless sacrifice—all they had to sacrifice was going without, while patting themselves on the back for being noble in accepting the things jfk would give 'em. (maybe a parallel in creative consumption?) HEY—DEVELOP THIS

a posture of concern can cover a hard line pretty effectively. the old idea of reluctant hard line, of the agonizing necessity of doing the unpalatable.

We're playing between Big Daddy and Super-Square, with the silent guru of the Hudson watching from his palisades.

keep hitting at the possibilities of power, at the opportunities it offers—at the things that have yet to be done. talk about 'em now as goals, while ducking means of reaching the goals—so as to build a sense of concern, assuming that most people assume that RN knows how to make a government work. Show a primary interest, though, in the uses of power rather than the techniques of its acquisition.

Voters are basically lazy, basically uninterested in making an *effort* to understand what we're talking about—even though they're interested in politics and feel a proprietary sense about the office of the Presidency. It takes effort to follow a logical argument. It takes an act of will to make the mind move in linear, logical paths

a shotgun approach—a package of pellets

we've got to appear larger than life, and this is one great advantage of a film: it can be projected larger than life.

yet always something in reserve, something they have to reach out for.

a sense of moving easily through and a bit above the crowd.

we can't win the election of 1968 with the techniques of 1952. We're not only in a television age, but in a television-*conditioned* age—and it's one of unease, of discontent, of frustration, largely undirected or multidirectional, diffuse—as it naturally would be in a suffusing environment. The environment itself is non-directional, and so is the common thought process. Thus a simple, directional logic won't do.

Use a directional logic to appeal to the directional thinkers—to those, like the columnists and commentators, whose whole professional life is devoted to the use of disciplined, directional, linear-verbal logic. And this is important; these are the men who filter the image and deliver it to the voters. It's what they say *about* the candidate that determines how the voter responds; after all, the voter wants to be fashionable, he wants to be seen thinking approved thoughts. (Even the rebels are desperate for the approval of their fellow-rebels; it's probably no accident that conformity is most rigid among the self-proclaimed non-conformists.)

Humor becomes vital; it cuts through the veils of logic, and shows a human side. It's appealing, democratic, communicative, in the sense of linking the two in a shared experience (i.e., a laugh, which is shared).

Q&A sessions yes; the performance is impressive, and gives a measure of the man.

spin out the bit about language and linear thinking, the processes of translation and re-translation, the effects of TV as a deconditioning medium—out of training.

It's probably not only the young, post-TV generation that is affected by this change in the primary way in which we get our informational inputs. To the extent that the older generation has grown accustomed to TV-type inputs, it too has probably been affected. It always is easier to unlearn than to learn a difficult discipline; we quickly grow flabby when our muscles fall into disuse. Logical, linear thinking is not a natural human characteristic. It is a learned response to a particular environment: in this case the environment of words, and of writing. The spoken word is linear, but it is not so elaborately or so meticulously structured as is the written word. (compare today's art forms and today's poetry—free verse, stream-of-consciousness writing, abstract expressionism. these don't follow linear logic, but rather barrage the audience with a shotgun burst of impressions.) However much care may have gone into their construction, the impression is one of carelessness, of randomness, of being everywhere-at-once.

Very few speakers speak in sentences that march as "cleanly" as those on the written page. They twist and turn and wrap themselves around a subject, subordinating the structure of the thought to its essence.

McLuhan tells us the new television environment takes us back to something like the old tribal balance of the senses; this is what he means when he says the world is becoming a global village. The sense of hearing is once more dominant. And among the characteristics of the "village," of the tribal milieu, are a heightened emotionalism, a susceptibility to rumor, a more unified, in the sense of de-specialized, existence. People who get their information by ear are more dependent on what they are told, and in the telling they get it with the extra dimension of inflection—the emotional overlay that the voice can give, but the printed word cannot.

Print converts abstractions into orderly, visible symbols, which march in a controlled and predetermined direction; and these symbols can be divided into categories. Print caused an "explosion," breaking society up into categories; the electronic media are causing an "implosion," forcing these categories back together again.

in the last 40 years, we've only had two elections in which the incumbent President was not running; in both of those, the out party won. (since 1928, when the in party won.) In the seven elections in which the incumbent was running, he lost only in 1932. But LBJ is only the second President in our history to ask for more than eight years in office, and only the second to run twice as an incumbent.

charisma: elements.

a sense of rapport, of touching across a gulf—of touching one's aspirations. There's a tactile quality here, somewhere, in a transubstantiated way. the lord's supper, that gory feast; the mystical communion—cannibalistic

he knows where the future lies   the way to the future not just new, but better   toward a better america in a bigger world

the idea of growth, that these years since 1960 have been spent in a mellowing and maturing and reflecting on the lessons of a life of massive involvement at the center of public affairs. so that now he comes to the job fresh. with spark, zest, assurance. not troubled yet with details, but clear about directions. details can wait; he doesn't have to prove himself on this as a newcomer would. he's already established himself as presidentabile. a bouncing back eager for the job, eager to get on with the unfinished business, summoning the nation to the urgencies of its tasks, urgencies now clearly seen from the vantage-point of the outside. like mcluhan's environments; you have to get outside it to see it. and now, having seen it from that vantage-point, he's eager to get back and start doing. convey a sense of restless energy, a chained beast, straining at the leash, eager not for combat but for the accomplishment that follows the combat.

the loser image—it's partly because of the habits of the press, always attaching the twice-lost label until it becomes practically a part of the name; but also because to a lot of people he just doesn't *feel* like a winner. It's not a rational thing, it's emotional; it's not thought out, it's felt. It's a response to the image they have of him as a personality—and that image is, to a lot, a person who may be admirable but isn't particularly likeable. They've seen the workaday RN, not the human RN, the machine, not the man. And the image is still two-dimensional and black-and-white; we've got to make it three-dimensional and color.

The black-and-white image: Probably to 99 voters out of 100, RN is a black-and-white image. He simply doesn't exist in color. Even if they've seen color photographs of him in magazines, these have been lost in the welter of black-and-white images—on newscasts, in the newspapers (where it's not only black-and-white but grainy). I still remember how stunned I was the first time I saw Kennedy in person, after his election—when he came striding into the State Department auditorium, and I saw that his hair was sandy-colored. I *knew* it was black, because that was the color it was in all those black-and-white images that filled my mind. And somehow this discovery threw my whole conception of the guy out of whack; since this thing I'd known wasn't true, how much else that I also knew might not be true? In this case, the truth somehow added a new dimension—and the same can happen if we can replace the black-and-white image of RN with a color image.

back to charisma: the tactile bit; LBJ puts great store in his "pressing the flesh," establishing physical contact with as many thousands of people as he can. It probably works; what we've got to devise is a workable substitute, that can accomplish the same thing wholesale that he does more or less retail. The film is one device, especially when it can be accompanied by Wilkinson and/or one of the girls. The physical presence of someone close to the candidate can bridge the space between the screen and the audience.

build up a mosaic; the tv generation thinks in mosaic terms, it receives mosaic impressions.

we've got to find a way to overleap LBJ—and the only way to do that is to direct our whole focus at the future, not the present. He bestrides the present; we can't compete with him on that ground. But we can compete with him for the future. We give him the '60s, and we ask for the '70s. We attack him on the '60s only in so far as it relates to the mandate for the '70s; otherwise we're not interested. JOHNSON IS THE PRESIDENT FOR THE '60s: RN THE PRESIDENT FOR THE '70s.

this, basically, would seem to be a rational and a linear thing; we've got to translate it into emotional and diffused terms. The key: the image of tomorrowness, of a contemporaneity that can leap over the fence of today, landing secure in tomorrow, and bridging past and future.

these are ongoing thoughts, fragments of the moment

we don't want tv exposure for exposure's sake, but we do want it: a) to establish a sense of hereness, of presence, in the primary states—the physical contact again, the sense of communion, and b) when we've got a chance to lay a new image over the old one, to help erase some of the familiar negatives and substitute some fresh positives. The one thing we mustn't do is give the viewers the chance to shake their heads and say, "See, it's the same old Nixon." WHEN ON TV, STAY AWAY FROM THE CLICHES OF THE '50S; KEEP THE FOCUS ON THE '60S AND '70S. KEEP THE FOCUS ON THE CHANGES THERE HAVE BEEN IN THE WORLD, AND THE VASTLY GREATER CHANGES WE HAVE TO PREPARE FOR. KEEP THE THRUST FORWARD, IN MOTION, NOT STOPPING. convey a sense of impatience with LBJ, a man who's got a lot on the ball but just doesn't have the vision of the future. who hasn't been able entirely to outlive his roots in the New Deal '30s.

One thing all this means is that, on TV, we should occasionally pause, grope—*involve* the viewer in the search for the right word or thought, share with him the participatory process of TV-watching. And, in this case, achieve that greater identification, the transubstantiation, absorbing him into our side of the fence.

What we're talking about here isn't so much a new image as it is a new use of the medium, a use better attuned to its own shortcomings and advantages and, more particularly, to the peculiar ways in which it gets to the people watching.

avoid reaching out for the pejorative example that's only dragged in to make a point (i.e. on evils of socialism)

mcluhan may be all wet on differences between TV and film; his talk of 2–3 million images on a TV screen vs twice as many or more in movies, and his insistence that these come out at the viewer on tv (i.e. light through) vs sitting there on the screen in movies (i.e. light on) doesn't seem significant. What may be more significant, in terms of social effect, is that movies were an occasional entertainment device, not the primary informational input; there wasn't the constant exposure there is with TV; they weren't really an environment, the way TV is. We didn't get into them the way we get into TV, as an ordinary part of the day's life. they required more of a conscious act, an effort, and they were outside the daily stream of experience rather than within it; moreover, they primarily were not reality programming, but escapism (though for most people tv is primarily escapism, probably—but is it possible that the line between reality and escape is less clearly drawn on TV, and that this itself has great significance for its political use?)

gotta electrify 'em. max frankel piece 11/20 on the malaise throughout the northeast—unstructured, unspecified, just general dissatisfaction somewhere below the rational surface. may be connected to the vacuum in the office of chief of state. to the eruptions of power where there oughtn't to be any—i.e. student power; to the fragmenting and fracturing of power, to the shifts from persuasion to force, suggesting that the whole fabric of society itself is being shredded.

A democratic society depends on debate, on free discussion, on common consent, on the submergence of individual differences in the common good. At least in our American experience, it typically takes the form of working through the two-party system, so that there's a double submergence; we agree to go along with things we don't entirely accept because we recognize them as the nearest obtainable to what we want. This is the only way, short of tyranny, that there can be stability.

But now we've got a system in which each person seems to feel entitled to have everything his own way—a rule-or-ruin mentality, which, on a broad scale, can only mean ruin since 200 million can't individually rule. It's divisive, discordant, raucous, shrill—and it's difficult to see any end to it other than suppression or tyranny. When the rebels insist on an all-or-nothing confrontation, society has to suppress them unless it's to cave in itself. If they won't accept integration into society; if they won't compromise; if they won't listen as the price of being listened to, then there's no place for them in a free society.

It galls us to have to do this. But students who come to a university for the apparent purpose of destroying it, ought to be sent packing. The university is there to educate; when they're ready to seek an education, let them come back.

COVERAGE: try substituting the stroll for the press conference; say that there won't be any formal press conference, but he wants to see a bit of the town and press are welcome to come along on the walk.

it's not important that we get coverage for the sake of coverage —that is, to get his name in the papers or to get across any particular thing that he's saying. But it IS important that we get across the idea that he was *there*. Here in New York we're used to having big wheels come to us; out in corn country, it's a big event. But you don't get that feeling of location in a press conference in a hotel room, or in an interview in the studios of the local TV station. These might have been done anywhere; ditto at the airport; airports are pretty much all alike. So get him out in the streets, in front of some landmarks; and have him walking, so that the cameras are *forced* to get the interesting angles, the sense of motion, etc. It's also bound to be looser, informal without being undignified; and if somebody rushes up to shake his hand, so much the better. Let him ask some questions, too—what's that over there type of thing, a few questions about the city itself, its people, so that it's give-and-take, interested, inquiring, and all in front of the cameras. This is also going to give the stations some more interesting footage than just the stock answers to the stock questions in the stock setting. Show that he's not only interested enough to *come* to Sheboygan, but that he wants to learn a little about Sheboygan, too; establish rapport, identification.

Why Richard Nixon Should Utilize Magazine Advertising in the State of New Hampshire Primary

HARRY TRELEAVEN

1. Generally, it has been agreed that the success of Richard Nixon's advertising effort in the primaries will depend importantly on the selection of the media which will carry his advertisements. However, to date, it appears that the selection of Nixon media has been governed strictly by the merits of reaching prospects at the lowest possible cost. What is more important than media reach or media efficiencies, is the editorial environment and the prestige environment of a given medium as it relates to Mr. Nixon's current image.

2. Generally, it has been agreed that all advertising for Mr. Nixon must communicate his *acceptability* to the masses. This "acceptability factor" is considered a very important element in persuading voters that he is the man qualified by far. Futhermore, it is agreed that Mr. Nixon's acceptability is currently an open question. It is an open and unanswered question because he is not always loved, he is not particularly glamourous, and he has been depicted as cold, objective and, even, ruthless.

The writer contends that a change in currently planned media strategy for the primaries will enhance significantly the opportunity to increase Mr. Nixon's acceptability. The writer proposes that a portion of the Nixon television budget be transferred to purchase regional editions of national magazines.

The writer believes firmly that the chances of overcoming Richard Nixon's cold image and the chances of *making* him loved and *making* him glamourous via commercial exposure on television (where admittedly he has not been at his best) are far less than the chances of *making* him loved and *making* him glamourous via saturation exposure of artfully conceived and produced four-color, full-page (or double spread) magazine advertisements.

These prestige advertisements will appear in mass circulation magazines like *Life* and *Look,* and more importantly, in the women's service books like *McCall's* and *Ladies' Home Journal.* There are more women voters in the United States than there are men voters. Are women going to vote for a Richard Nixon they currently believe to be cold, unloving, unglamourous? No. Can the most artfully conceived thirty-second or sixty-second television commercial change this long term image? The writer believes probably not because of the limitations of the TV medium in terms of:

    a) The environment of entertainment that precludes serious character portrayal and
    b) The time limitation of a sixty-second or thirty-second commercial.

But, rich, warm advertising in a woman's own medium, the service magazine, next to her cake mixes and her lipstick advertisement will go a long way, I believe, toward making Mr. Nixon acceptable to female viewers. In addition, people tend to discredit television as a "vast wasteland" and the "boob tube." Mr. Nixon's TV commercials will suffer in credibility because of this unfavorable environment. On the other hand, the editorial environment of prestigious magazines is beyond question and will indirectly serve as an endorsement for the candidate.

Warm, human, four-color magazine illustrations depicting Dick Nixon the family man, perhaps even surrounded by his beautiful family, will allow the women of America, and initially, the women of New Hampshire, to identify with him, and his home life. This exposure will break down the current cold barrier he projects to women. This warm visual image will be supported by strong reader copy that, point by point, will sell his qualifications to voters who can study the advertisement leisurely in their home. This kind of reader copy is ideally suited toward fully supporting Mr. Nixon's qualifications: experience, knowledgeability, intellectual ability, acceptability, ability to form a top team, toughness, integrity, and conscientiousness.

This type of reader copy advertising can only serve to complement the fleeting visual impressions which will be left by his thirty-second and sixty-second television commercials.

Additionally, Mr. Nixon's magazine advertising will be unique in the medium. Have you ever seen a political advertisement in a magazine?

When a major manufacturer wants to introduce his new product in the most glamourous setting and register the product in the most appealing fashion, what medium does he utilize? He utilizes the medium with the most "appetite appeal": four-color magazine advertising.

In addition to the quality reasons why Nixon advertising must include magazine exposure, the cost is cheap. A full-page four-color advertisement in the New Hampshire edition of *Life* magazine costs only $1,475. Similar costs are available for other magazines and these magazines will accept political advertising provided they have the right to review copy.

Because regional closings are far in advance of issue dates, the time to act is now. Advertisements must be created, engravings completed and materials sent to the publications.

If all materials are ready by late-December, an effective list of magazines utilizing regional editions could be implemented for the New Hampshire primary.

Time is growing short. This proposal is important—one of the most important factors in Mr. Nixon's advertising campaign. The time to act is now.

An Outline of Strategy

PATRICK K. BUCHANAN

The polls today show RN leading by a sizable margin in N.H.; Governor Romney is the one who must play "hurry-up" football. What sort of strategy should we map out now—for N.H.

1) I would *right now lock into only the minimum necessary appearances in N.H., essential to holding our lead,* and considering that George will campaign heavily. We must schedule enough so that Romney camp cannot argue "Only George Cared Enough to Come," and we *must not schedule so much* as to risk overexposure, to risk boring the electorate, so that the Hampshireites, weary with the contentious disputants, follow their own arbitrary natures and write-in someone.

We should thus lock in only a necessary minimum—in terms of both tv and speeches and appearances. What is that minimum?

2) The Nixon Coalition in N.H. right now (a guess) consists of 40 percent Republican Regulars, 40 percent conservative Republicans, and 20 percent moderates and liberals who think Rocky is out, Romney is out to lunch, and Reagan would be a disaster.

From the polls, from the reports we get, from the Ploesser memos, we get this reading on the Nixon coalition. Almost to a man it believes RN is the best qualified man to be President, most capable in foreign policy, most capable on the issues. There is widespread concern through this coalition that a) RN is a loser, and b) he cannot generate sufficient enthusiasm and excitement.

The points immediately above indicate to me *the necessity to do more traditional campaigning than was envisioned in that New York Times story saying we would give lofty speeches,* get in and out of the State. They already think we are the smartest candidate; what the majority want to know is can we win—and we can't convince them of this by talking about Vietnam and the Middle East.

In Wisconsin, we will have the victory in N.H. to show we are winners—In New Hampshire, *we must have winner written all over us.*

We have said *minimum essential appearances.* Now, what kind? First, we should give those lofty speeches on foreign policy which show our superiority over the opposition in clear terms. Such speeches as will re-inforce (we don't need to create the impression; it is already there) the concept of the great majority that we know more than anybody else what we are talking about. Thus, we "flash" our credentials of ability, experience and knowledge— while Romney has to have his inspected at great length.

Then, to hammer the loser thing (at the same time we dispel the myths of RN being tough and mean and political and intense), we use the tv to show everyone in New Hampshire that RN is enjoying the hell out of this campaign. He is smiling, confident, easy-going (no cornball stuff) comes off well in "feature" settings, with kids, with folks etc. In short, while RN talks like the President-in-Exile, he is a good democrat (with a small d) who believes that communicating with the people is one of the great joys of seeking the Presidency.

While our mail advertising ought to be providing polls and every other thing we can to hit the loser thing—*RN's attitude* as much as anything else will create the impression of a rolling bandwagon. (One thing we have going for us is that if Romney stays behind he may get George Christopher-like, testy, irritable and bitchy and those are the sure marks of a drowning candidate. They won't be missed by tv eye or press either.)

That is the kind of tv we do want. Our controlled ads, RN smiling when campaigning, RN the Statesman when speaking. We don't need any press conference type stuff where RN is being baited by reporters and saying why he would oppose the rat control bill or something. We just don't need that; and it should be considered a necessary evil when we have to have it.

3) Basic Strategy then: First class printed advertising, first class filmed spots and films of RN, plus friends and the surrogates of RN *should carry the message into N.H. and bear the brunt of the campaign against George—while RN himself waits in reserve, watching the progress of the conflict. RN only does what is neces-*

sary and essential. If George fails to move in the polls, if he puts his shoe in his mouth a few times, we follow the same strategy. If he starts moving rapidly upward, we then start closing some of the options we left open—we start locking in to telethons perhaps; we start campaigning in earnest.

However, while RN has a schedule perhaps half that of Romney, our people ought to have the line out that RN has determined to do whatever is necesary to get his message across to the people of N.H., to go into the towns if need be and the city halls etc. We will consider it an all-out campaign. That might well be the line.

4) Romney Strategy. All-out street corner effort certainly. Also, the necessity to talk a great deal on the issues to convince the people he can handle them. The press will be picking him apart on issues and specifics if he tries to duck them. *If by three weeks before the election Romney has not moved up considerably in the polls—I would imagine a direct challenge would come to RN.* Romney might well grab one end of an issue—of which RN held the other—and then try to have the election decided on it. Perhaps it might be Vietnam.

We should avoid this at all costs. If it's decided on the best man and qualifications, we win; so let's avoid having it settled on the single issue. We ought to ignore challenges to debate; we are running against LBJ not George Romney—*voters should choose who is better qualified, who can make a better case, who can win.* We should avoid locking horns or getting into comparative situations with Romney.

(I have heard that it is expected that RN and Romney both will be on Meet the Press the day before election (rather the Sunday before) I would skip this drill, if we are well ahead.)

(If we bump into George and we can't avoid it, we ought to play the JFK bit, when Johnson kept demanding he debate at the 1960 Democratic convention. If we are getting heat, we might pop in unexpectedly on Romney somewhere, take the floor, and give them about ten minutes of what needs to be changed in America, high-level, then say the Republican Party can provide that leadership. Within this party there are the human resources "to turn America around into the proper path of her destiny. We have great Governors like George Romney and Senators like your own Norris Cotton. We will win if we stand together, and I say right here If Governor Romney gets that nomination, he will have no more loyal supporter than me." This type of drill, where there is no contest, no grappling of arms to wrestle.

5) ISSUES. It has been argued that RN should take a thematic approach, give his philosophy, tell what is wrong with America, point out the direction of the new solution, and perhaps a few major programs might be broadly defined. This is fine; and it avoids the petty issues that divide men. But the press will not let us get away with it; and for them RN should be thoroughly briefed on the major issues of the day, with statistics and facts and phrases for the press conferences. While we might not want to get into the nitty-gritty, RN should be prepared for it. There is no need to antagonize the press by staying off of some issues RN is pressed on. RN has never had problems in this area, and he ought to level with the press. As one earlier memo said, RN's demonstration not only of convictions, but of tremendous knowledge and ability will be sharply contrasted in these writer's minds with George—and the contrast may be reflected in their stories.

Because of the nature of our coalition (conservative personally or politically) in N.H., we ought not to come up there and jolt their current impression of RN as Mr. Solid. Republican progressive is a good posture. *Even if we are going to come out for something like the negative income tax, it ought to be delayed until after this type of thing is over.*

However, I would agree with Ray that we ought not, when in N.H., lock the door to any proposal that might be worthwhile nationally later.

6) STRATEGY BETWEEN NOW AND NEW HAMPSHIRE. Our national coalition is similar to that in New Hampshire; and to cement it the same rules apply. Demonstrate we can generate enthusiasm and excitement; demonstrate (partly through the primaries and partly in attitude) that we are a winner; demonstrate (again, just re-inforce impressions rather than create them) that . . . we are by far the best qualified.

Thus, rather than political reporters walking through the office, I would like to see an AP feature writer maybe and some (friendly only) magazine writers. (As for the political reporters, they should be sent away with the message of RN, by no means overconfident, but cool, calm, confident and fatalistic.)

We would like to see some more (not very much) tv of RN, with the accent on destroying the old myths. Also, perhaps some press feature shots (again not overdone) of RN on a golf course or something that is legitimate feature without being cornball or contrived.

We could use some more feature stuff on the youth of the Staff, and the idea merchants etc. We ought to get the Draft piece around to youth of the country. We ought to be thinking in terms of material that will make points with the Negro. These people are not locked into LBJ; they are not particularly hostile to RN; they are indifferent to RN, and maybe some of them can be sold on RN.

On this feature stuff—whether tv or press or photos or situation —it ought to be such so as to *surprise* someone who has a stereotype of RN, but not *so* much as to make him think it is contrived.

What was ideal about the Carson thing was that it did three things in one.

First, RN with his very brief and articulate piece on "world peace" re-inforced the notion of his ability in world affairs; then with the needle about the "ten tickets" and the other gave the lie to the impression that RN is humorless—then with the girls, this tore into the mean and dispassionate image.

Notes on Television Advertising
in New Hampshire

HARRY TRELEAVEN

December 18, 1967

The objectives of the 60- and 30-second television spots will be to:

1. Attack the loser image by emphasizing the electability of Richard Nixon. This will be done with endorsements by well known and respected New Hampshire citizens; by publicizing favorable out-of-state poll results; and by frequently showing a smiling and confident candidate surrounded by enthusiastic supporters.

2. Remind voters of Mr. Nixon's unique qualifications, with emphasis on his experience in foreign affairs and his Washington background.

3. Remind voters that this is a "troubled, dangerous time," that we need a man like Nixon now.

4. Hit hard at our theme—"Nixon's the One!"—by using it to pay off every commercial message.

The shorter lengths are well suited to accomplish these objectives. However, they are less suited as a vehicle for examining issues, or for presenting Nixon in depth, or for showing him in an interacting relationship with voters. For these objectives we will use a series of 5-minute "programs"—one a night on three stations for the last 14 nights of the campaign.

Each 5-minute segment will show Nixon (and/or members of his family) in a discussion situation with a specific group of voters, which will vary from program to program. One night he'll be with a general mixed group in a town meeting situation; the next night with a college group; the next with veterans; etc. The exact format may change slightly, but in general it will be as follows:

We open as if we'd walked in late, in the middle of a question. As Nixon starts to answer, a voice over announcer identifies the program and a super comes on (suggested titles: "Hotseat"; "Nixon on the spot"; "Nixon speaks up on what's getting you down"; "Dialogues with Richard Nixon"; "Straight talk"; "Nixon in New Hampshire"; etc.). The group is identified. And for the rest of the period, the program is simply an informal unrehearsed question and answer session between Nixon and the group. The setting will be casual and the mood easy. There will be humor, seriousness, provocativenes, controversy and sincerity. The plan would be to tape 20 or 30 minutes of discussion, then edit it down to the most interesting 5 minutes. Questions would be planted to make sure that the issues we want discussed would be brought up.

We should consider placing tune-in ads every day which would give the time and stations of that evening's program. We should also quote the programs in daily news releases; in other words, use them to generate news.

A few suggested groups for these programs:

1. General town meeting
2. Nixon meets youth (perhaps with his daughters)
3. Nixon and Vietnam veterans
4. Nixon and the press
5. *Mrs.* Nixon and the ladies
6. Nixon and the Republican leaders
7. Nixon on the farm
8. The Nixon family and some early Americana
9. Nixon visits local industry
10. Nixon meets New Hampshire businessmen
    Etc.

On the Sunday preceding the election a two-hour telethon is planned. Details for this will be worked out later. There will also be a 30-minute program on election eve, which will probably feature a film dramatizing the comeback aspect of Nixon's candidacy.

Notes re Oregon RNFP Advertising

HARRY TRELEAVEN

May, 1968

The situation: Primary day is May 28. No cross-over vote. Independents a negligible factor. Reagan on the ballot but has no plans to campaign personally in the state; however, an estimated $350,000 will be spent to promote his candidacy—probably mostly on television. Nixon can be expected to match this. A Rockefeller write-in is possible but will be small.

Reagan's strategy will probably emphasize three things: his personal attractiveness; his conservatism—anti-big government, anti-big spending, with special stress on his economy moves in California; and his ability to win. It's anybody's guess how much he'll push his hard-line hawk position on Vietnam; he's probably waiting to see how the negotiations go.

In a way, McCarthy and Kennedy are helping Reagan by injecting an excitement and an appeal to youth that may make RN seem drab by contrast. Voters who might ordinarily back Nixon may swing to Reagan for impractical, emotional reasons—just so they can feel as with it as the Democrats.

There's little doubt that RN will win in Oregon. The objective is to get a big percentage of a big turn-out.

Strategy: We still have to convince a lot of voters that RN can win. People were just getting convinced he could beat LBJ when March 31 happened. Now, according to the latest Harris Poll, they have to be convinced he can beat RFK or McCarthy. Not quite as easy—particularly among the younger voters. And the advertising can't push RN's winability too obviously or it will seem defensive.

Our wins in New Hampshire, Wisconsin and Nebraska should, of course, be exploited (plus the fact that he entered them—people like a man who *tries*). More than ever it's important that the advertising have an upbeat, optimistic mood—contemporary in feeling yet, as in the New Hampshire strategy, appropriate to a presidential campaign.

We should continue to stress our exclusive advantages: RN's experience in Washington and abroad, his knowledge of foreign affairs, etc.—"The one man better prepared for the presidency than any other challenger in history."—"The only man with the experience, knowledge, etc. to lead the country, etc."

Perhaps the experience and qualifications aspect could be tied to the wins in the other states—as the reason for his victories. "More and more thinking Republicans recognize that RN etc., etc."

We should not let Reagan pre-empt the anti-big government position. RN is pretty conservative in this area, too.

Item: The biggest hand RN's been getting has been when he talks about people having more respect for law and order.

Item: most people still don't know RN was a highly successful lawyer between 1960 and the present.

Thought starters: What could we do using RN voice over scenes depicting an area of current interest? In the Hillsboro tapes we have ready-made narration on just about every subject, from youth—"it's an exciting time to be alive"—to inflation—"we must make sure that the dollar you save today is still worth a dollar when you retire." This will require a reading of the transcripts.

A commercial which tells the story of the primaries—perhaps starting with RN's Hillsboro comment on the necessity for a candidate to go to the people and discuss the issues head-on—then show scenes of RN in the various states—"and the people responded overwhelmingly."

Would Hillsboro quotes be useable in a newspaper ad? How could we use daytime-TV? (There's a good interview with Pat Nixon in the documentary.)

Should we try a commercial which shows Nixon in a series of crowd situations—full of smiles and waves and victory—cut to a strong lively music track?

Is there a new way to do an endorsement commercial?

How could we get at the issues by showing *positives?*

Notes re Recruiting Panels for
Question and Answer Tapings

FULLER AND SMITH
AND ROSS OFFICE MEMORANDUM

June 26, 1968

Next Monday morning, July 1, we will tape a question-and-answer session with Mr. Nixon and a small group of Illinois and Michigan citizens. This tape will be shown the following week on television stations throughout Illinois.

Because of the candidate's schedule, the taping must be done here. Therefore, it will be necessary to fly the Illinois group to New York.

We need your help in recruiting the group. Here is what we want specifically:

Six people, residents of Illinois, from as many different parts of the state as possible. Three could be from the Chicago area, but no more.

The group should have a young look. Try to stick close to these ages: three 25–35; three 35–50, preferably around 40.

Four men and two women, or three and three.

They should be reasonably attractive, white—representative of the average middle-class voter.

Most importantly, they should be intelligent, articulate, well informed, and interested in current affairs. With a few questions, you should be able to establish their awareness of today's issues: crime, race problems, inflation, taxes, Vietnam, rioting, etc. They don't have to be experts—just have a reasonable knowledge of what's going on and a concern about the situation. They do not necessarily have to be Nixon supporters. In fact, it's desirable that some of the participants be uncommitted—or leaning in another direction—just so they're not actually hostile.

They should not be directly associated with the Nixon campaign, or in politics as an office-holder or candidate. Find business and professional people, housewives, etc. Look for extroverts who will not be intimidated by a television studio environment. There will be no studio audience; nevertheless, we want to be careful we don't recruit anybody who'll freeze in front of the camera.

We will pay for a round-trip, first-class plane ticket, two nights in a New York hotel, and all meals and miscellaneous expenses while the participant is in New York.

The procedure will be this: Participants may fly to New York any time this week-end—but they must be checked in at the hotel (address) by Six p.m. Sunday evening. A representative of the Nixon organization will contact them between six and seven with specific instructions for the next day's taping, so they should be in their rooms during that hour and wait for the call.

On Monday morning, they will be picked up at the hotel and driven to the studio. Men should wear suits or conservative sportcoat and tie; women should wear daytime dress or suit. Before the taping, the group will be thoroughly briefed on the routine—but will *not* be given specific questions to ask. Therefore, participants should have several questions in mind before they arrive. A thorough reading of the Sunday New York Times and the latest issues of the U. S. News and World Report, Time and Newsweek is recommended.

If there are any problems between now and Sunday at six, they should call Bill Coldus (212) 765-4321 or Al Scott (212) 355-7934

Notes re NFP Advertising—Phase One

HARRY TRELEAVEN

July 15, 1968

Phase One is the period between the Republican Convention and that time when the opponent's strategy is known and we can plan our counter strategy—probably early in September. This does not necessarily mean a shift in strategy in September; hopefully, most of the advertising we produce now will continue through the fall. However, we should re-examine our approach constantly as the opposition's program develops.

Since these are notes and not a formal strategy paper, the following points may appear somewhat random. Nevertheless, they all are important to our Phase One effort.

It is my belief that the most effective posture for Mr. Nixon is that of *challenger*—which means, of course, that we always regard Mr. Humphrey as a key member of the incumbent administration, sharing responsibility for past and present policies and committed to their continuation in the years ahead. While this may not be entirely true, and will certainly be argued by Mr. Humphrey as he attempts to establish his individuality, it must be the basis for our strategy.

Expanding the above, we must convince the public that HH is tied to the past, to policies that don't work, and that he stands for more of the same. More crises. More confusion. More wars. More inflation. More lawlessness. More loss of respect for the U.S. abroad. RN, on the other hand, stands for *change*. For new ideas,

233

positive action, imaginative, workable programs that will help solve the problems now plagueing us.

Corollary to the above: we must play on the importance and frustration of today's voters. They *want* change. They may not yet agree that Richard Nixon is the man who can make it happen—that's our job. But the people are certainly ready to listen and be convinced. And it doesn't seem to be a time for subtlety, rather, we should be direct, and inject a note of urgency into our approach. It *is* a time of crisis—and people should be reminded of it.

Now to the heart of our problem; how do we convince people that Richard Nixon is the man who can effect the changes the country wants?

Two ways. First, we must overcome the negative anti-Nixon feeling that persists in so many minds. It is very difficult to get a man's opinions considered or even listened to if he is not liked. However, our experience in the primary campaigns showed us that we *can* change people's attitude toward Nixon—that most people don't really know what Nixon today looks and sounds like, and when they do, when they're shown the new Nixon, they start coming around to our side. Therefore, during Phase One at least, exposure of the 1968 Nixon is a first priority of the advertising.

The second way we can convince people that Nixon's the One is to present his stand on the important issues. Most people have only a vague idea of Nixon's position—many people have a distorted impression—few people know exactly where he stands. In fact, one of the things many people don't like about Nixon is that they consider him too general in his views—not evasive but unspecific and inclined to be self-serving in his statements. The facts belie this, of course—and letting the public know precisely the Nixon position is a major objective of the advertising.

This means we should immediately list the issues we want to deal with and the Nixon stand on each, phrased as succinctly as possible and *in terms that will have the most real meaning for the average voter.*

(Incidentally, the above should be done state by state, as the issues and emphases will probably vary.)

Getting back to building Nixon's acceptability—we should strongly consider the use of high-level endorsements. The opinion of someone you respect has more meaning than the most soundly constructed argument. This is the "prior approval" factor at work; *he* likes him, so maybe *I* would (or should). Two types of endorsements should be considered; well known national figures, such as John Wayne, Wilt Chamberlain, etc.—and popular local figures for use in one state. Lists of both and a sample format should be developed immediately.

The localization of the advertising (pinpointing the message) should include a special anti-Wallace effort in states where he can take a sizeable vote away from RN. It should not attack Wallace— that would have a negative effect because, whatever we think of him, he's well liked in those areas. One suggestion is to use Strom Thurmond in a special 60-second or 5-minute TV film.

Another special group which should get immediate attention is the daytime women's audience. Should we produce special spots for this audience? Programs? What about women's magazines? The female vote is large enough (and less tied to party loyalty— i.e., easier to change) to warrant its own campaign.

We must also re-examine our 5-minute program philosophy The 5-minute segment was used very effectively in New Hampshire and Oregon; it should be a basic part of our fall planning. One format we should consider is a series of "dialogues"—similar to the RN-Chamberlain conversation—between Nixon and various interesting personalities from sports, show business, politics, intellectual circles, etc.

A few guidelines for the advertising in general:

The style of the advertising must be appropriate—to the man, his background, and the office he is seeking. We are representing in our advertising a former Vice-President of the United States, a man with specific and well known personality traits, a candidate for the most important office in the world.

Cuteness, obliqueness, way-outness, slickness—any gimmicks that proclaim "Madison Avenue at work here" should be avoided. Imaginative approaches, contemporary techniques—yes. But beware of "over-creativity." The basic seriousness of our purpose, our *candor,* must show plainly in everything we do.

And let's make sure the groups we direct our messages to are where the votes are—and that the messages are truly meaningful. The Negro community, youth, etc., are tempting targets—but that's not where *this* game will be won.

In our search for a new theme, let's not be too quick to discard the old one: "There's one man today who stands for a new order—who believes in America and etc., etc., Nixon's the One!"

It seems this would be an easy line to research—in and out of an advertising contest. And that we should get a public reaction before deciding whether or not to replace it.

Any new line should come out of this proposition:

Things aren't right. And they're going to get worse because the programs and policies we have now aren't working.

A change is urgently needed. There's only one candidate who stands for change: Richard M. Nixon.

Notes re Nixon Advertising
after September 1

HARRY TRELEAVEN

Our advertising between Labor Day and the election will have two objectives:

1. To present *Nixon the Man* in ways that will dispel existing negative feelings about his personality and sincerity—that will show him as a knowledgeable, experienced, and likeable candidate. Our efforts in the primaries proved this to be an attainable objective. Now we must do more of what we know works, on a state, regional, and national basis.

2. To present the *Nixon stand* on the issues in provocative and compelling ways. We know his position on most issues have wide acceptance *when people learn what they are.* Millions of voters—including Democrats and Independents—are in a mood to agree with Nixon's solutions; it is a function of the advertising to communicate the RN position effectively. This is a far more important objective now than it was during the primary campaigns.

The following steps will be taken to implement the above:

1. We will plan and schedule a series of one-hour television rallies in as many of the key states as possible. Tentative format: establish location and event (lots of partisan cheering—an upbeat bandwagon atmosphere); 5–10 minute introductory remarks by RN; 40–45 minute question and answer session with a panel of editors, professors, business executives and other well-informed and articulate experts; 5–10 minutes of interviews with local celebrities as they leave the auditorium; and closing. *Although the programs will, of course, deal with issues, their principal objective*

will be to present Nixon the Man, *and to surround his candidacy with excitement and enthusiasm.*

2. From the above we will edit *5-minute segments* for local scheduling during the weeks following the one-hour telecast.

Note re 1 and 2: Because of the importance of these programs, it is recommended that a permanent team of producer, assistant producer, and writer-editor-coordinator be assigned exclusively to this project. In addition, a close liaison with PR is essential for effective pre-promotion and post-publicity activities.

3. We will immediately plan a series of *5-minute dialogues* between RN and nationally known leaders from business, publishing, intellectual groups, etc. (similar in format to the Wilt Chamberlain interview). These would be taped in New York—either in the apartment or on a set. In some instances these could have a local or regional slant (e.g., dialogues with Strom Thurmond, Reagan, etc. for use in the South; with Lindsay, Commissioner Leary, etc. for use in big cities—etc.). Procedure would be to shoot several—perhaps 8–10—in a day.

4. How can we follow up on the suggestion that we produce a Billy Graham program for use in the South?

5. Principal method of implementing our second objective—presenting *the Nixon stand* on issues—will be via 60- and 40-second television spots, 60- and 30-second radio spots, and full page newspaper ads.

6. It is hoped the newspaper ads can go into immediate production so that the first ad can run the Wednesday after Labor Day. This means approval of text and layout *no later than Tuesday, August 27.*

7. Several different kinds of television spots are being planned. . . .

The two series described above will take care of our *immediate* need for commercial material.

David Duncan has recommended two people—Eugene Jones and Raysa Bonow—as extremely talented producers of the kind of thing Duncan did in Miami Beach—the documentary treatment of a subject through imaginative use of still photographs. Both have been contacted, both are interested (whether they should work together or separately has yet to be determined) and we would like to get them both started immediately on an *experimental series* of commercials. There are three areas they should explore: the Nixon stand on issues; Nixon the man; and the Nixon philosophy (moral decay of youth, are we a sick society? the face of a child, etc.). Both short (60- and 40-second) and 5-minute spots will be produced. This experimenting will be expensive, but hopefully will result in some highly unusual treatment that will enhance the campaign.

Experimenting will also get underway on a series of strong anti-administration and anti-Humphrey spots.

8. As an aid in developing advertising in all media—and pinpointing specific local problems and/or opportunities, we must immediately establish communication with those who are directing individual state and regional efforts. We need one man in each key state who can advise us on a *continuing* basis. Do we have a state by state political strategy? Do we need a special campaign for the South?

9. Is there any merit in a plan for a series of weekly 5-minute radio and TV shows in which RN would comment on the week's events—give his views on the news, what *he* would do, his personal analysis of the situation, etc.?

SCRIPTS

On the pages that follow are the complete scripts of a representative sampling of the spot commercials made by E.S.J. Productions, Inc., for Richard Nixon.

TWO VERSIONS:
:60 seconds
:40 seconds

E.S.J. #2
"ORDER"

VIDEO	AUDIO
1. OPENING NETWORK DISCLAIMER: "A POLITICAL ANNOUNCEMENT."	
2. FADEUP ON RAPIDLY MOVING SEQUENCE OF RIOTING, URBAN MOB MOTIVATING TO CROWDS TAUNTING POLICE AUTHORITIES.	SFX UP FULL. SFX UNDER.
3. FLAMING APT. HOUSE DISSOLVING TO POLICE PATROLLING DESERTED STREETS IN AFTERMATH OF VIOLENCE.	R.N. It is time for some honest talk about the problem of order in the United States.
4. PERPLEXED FACES OF AMERICANS.	R.N. Dissent is a necessary ingredient of change. But in a system of government that provides for peaceful change—

VIDEO

AUDIO

5. SEQUENCE OF SHOTS OF PEOPLE MOVING THROUGH BATTERED STREETS ORDERED BY DESTROYED SHOPS AND HOMES.

—there is no cause that justifies resort to violence. There is no cause that justifies rule by mob instead of by reason.

6. ELOQUENT FACES OF AMERICANS WHO HAVE LIVED THROUGH SUCH EXPERIENCES, CLIMAXED BY SINGLE SHOT OF CHARRED CROSSBEAMS FRAMING A RIOT RUIN. IN CENTER OF PICTURE IS BATTERED MACHINE ON WHICH CAN STILL BE SEEN IN RED LETTERS THE WORD "CHANGE." FADEOUT.

MUSIC UP AND OUT.

7. FADEUP TITLE: "THIS TIME VOTE LIKE YOUR WHOLE WORLD DE-PENDED ON IT."

8. DISSOLVE TO TITLE WORD "NIXON." ZOOM TO CU. HOLD. FADEOUT.

9. CLOSING NETWORK DIS-CLAIMER: "THE PRECED-ING PRE-RECORDED PO-LITICAL BROADCAST WAS PAID FOR BY THE NIXON-AGNEW CAMPAIGN COM-MITTEE."

THE SELLING OF THE PRESIDENT 1968

TWO VERSIONS:
:60 seconds
:40 seconds

E.S.J. #5
"CRIME"

VIDEO

AUDIO

1. OPENING NETWORK DIS-
CLAIMER: "A POLITICAL
ANNOUNCEMENT."

2. FADEUP ON PAN INTO
LONELY POLICEMAN AT
CALL BOX. MOTIVATE
SUDDENLY TO SERIES OF
SHOTS OF EXPLOSIVE
CRIMINAL ACTIONS WITH
POLICE RESPONSE END-
ING ON IMAGE OF A BUL-
LET-SHATTERED AUTO-
MOBILE WINDOW, WHICH
SPINS INTO A BLUR. DIS-
SOLVE. PAN UP ROW OF
WEAPONS—THEN CON-
TINUE TILT UP "KENNEDY
RIFLE" AND FINALLY TO
HUGE CU OF HAND
HOLDING AN OPEN JACK
KNIFE.

MUSIC UP AND UNDER.

MUSIC UNDER.
R.N.
In recent years crime in this country has grown nine times as fast
as the population. At the current
rate, the crimes of violence in
America will double by 1972. We
cannot accept that kind of future.

3. CUT TO MONTAGE OF
FACES OF AMERICANS.
THEY ARE ANXIOUS, PER-
PLEXED, FRIGHTENED.

We owe it to the decent and law-
abiding citizens of America to
take the offensive against the
criminal forces that threaten their
peace and security—

4. SEQUENTIAL STORY
BRIEFLY ILLUSTRATING
CRIMES THAT PLAGUE

—and to rebuild respect for law
across this country.

VIDEO   AUDIO

THE ORDINARY CITIZEN:
THE DILEMMA IMPOSED
UPON US BY INCREASE
OF DRUG SALES TO THE
YOUNG; VICTIM OF MUG-
GING; YOUTHS FIGHTING
POLICE; CAPTURE OF
ROBBERY SUSPECT BY PO-
LICE.

5. DOLLY IN MLS ON LINE   R.N.
OF HANDCUFFED CRIM-   I pledge to you that the wave of
INALS STANDING BY   crime is not going to be the wave
BRICK WALL, THEIR   of the future in America!
FACES CONCEALED BY
THEIR HANDS OR COATS.
FADEOUT.   MUSIC UP AND OUT.

6. FADEUP TITLE: "THIS
TIME VOTE LIKE YOUR
WHOLE WORLD DE-
PENDED ON IT."

7. DISSOLVE TO TITLE
WORD "NIXON." ZOOM IN-
TO CU. HOLD. FADEOUT.

8. CLOSING NETWORK DIS-
CLAIMER: "THE PRECED-
ING PRE-RECORDED PO-
LITICAL BROADCAST WAS
PAID FOR BY THE NIXON-
AGNEW CAMPAIGN COM-
MITTEE."

TWO VERSIONS:
:60 seconds
:40 seconds

E.S.J. #6
"WRONG ROAD"

VIDEO

AUDIO

1. OPENING NETWORK DIS-
CLAIMER: "A POLITICAL
ANNOUNCEMENT."

2. DOLLY DOWN LS EMPTY
ROAD ACROSS WESTERN
AREA. DISSOLVE TO
MATCH MOVEMENT PAN
—TILT IN ON DEJECTED
MAN ASLEEP ON PARK
BENCH. THEN INTO
SCENES OF BOTH URBAN
AND RURAL DECAY.

MUSIC UP AND UNDER.
R.N.
For the past five years we've been
deluged by programs for the un-
employed—programs for the cities—programs for the poor. And
we have reaped from these programs an ugly harvest of frustra-
tions, violence and failure across
the land.

3. MOTIVATES INTO SE-
QUENCE OF FACES OF
AMERICA—ALL RACES,
ALL BACKGROUNDS.
THERE IS A QUALITY OF
DETERMINATION TO
THEM, BUT THEY APPEAR
SORELY TRIED.

R.N.
Now our opponents will be offering more of the same. But I say
we are on the wrong road. It is
time to quit pouring billions of
dollars into programs that have
failed.

THEY ARE THE HUNGRY
OF APPALACHIA—THE
POOR OF AN URBAN
GHETTO—THE ILL-
HOUSED MEMBERS OF A
FAMILY ON AN INDIAN
RESERVATION. SLOWLY
BUT FIRMLY THE PIC-

VIDEO   AUDIO

TURE LEADS TOWARD A
SCENE OF FRUSTRATED
ANGER, WHICH IS EX-
PRESSED IN THEIR FACES.

SIGN ON STREETS WHICH   R.N.
SAYS, "GOVERNMENT   What we need are not more mil-
CHECKS CASHED HERE."   lions on welfare rolls—but more
                          people on payrolls in the United
                          States.

4. SERIES OF QUICK, EFFEC-   I believe we should enlist private
   TIVE CUTS OF CONSTRUC-   enterprise, which will produce,
   TIVE WORK SCENES—   not promises in solving the prob-
   A SHIP UNLOADING—A   lems of America.
   TOWER BEING RAISED—
   A FACTORY LINE—A
   BUILDING ERECTED.

5. DISSOLVE TO SHOT OF   MUSIC UP AND OUT.
   CHILDREN STANDING IN
   THE MUD OF APPALA-
   CHIA. THEY STARE AT
   THE CAMERA. TILT DOWN
   FOR MATCH MOVEMENT
   DISSOLVE TO SILO OF
   LITTLE NEGRO BOY
   (BACK TO CAMERA) AS
   HE LOOKS OUT WINDOW.
   HOLD. FADEOUT.

TWO VERSIONS:
:60 seconds
:40 seconds

E.S.J. #11
"A CHILD'S FACE"

VIDEO	AUDIO
1. OPENING NETWORK DIS-CLAIMER: "A POLITICAL ANNOUNCEMENT."	
2. PULLBACK FROM CU OF MOTHER AND TILT TO CHILD WITH DISSOLVE TO ECU OF LATTER.	MUSIC UP AND UNDER. R.N. I see the face of a child . . . What his color is . . . what his ancestry is, doesn't matter.
3. MONTAGE CHILDREN's FACES.	What does matter is he is an American child. That child is more important than any politician's promise.
4. BABIES INTO CHILD-HOOD AND THEN FROM YOUNG ADOLESCENCE INTO THE EXCITEMENT OF THE OUTER WORLD FOR A FROLIC.	MUSIC UP AND UNDER.
5. ESTABLISH WALL ON WHICH CHILD IS PAINT-ING BOTH WORDS AND SYMBOLS.	R.N. He is everything we have ever hoped to be and everything we dare to dream.
6. MONTAGE POOR CHIL-DREN.	R.N. This child must not have his dream become a living nightmare of poverty, neglect and despair.

VIDEO

AUDIO

He must not be the victim of a system that feeds his stomach but starves his soul.

7. FINAL SHOT OF CHILD AND MATCH TILT DISSOLVE INTO 2-SHOT OF CHILDREN STANDING AT EDGE OF POND. FADEOUT.

I ask you to help me make the American dream come true for those to whom it seems an impossible dream.
MUSIC UP AND OUT.

8. FADEUP TITLE: "THIS TIME VOTE LIKE YOUR WHOLE WORLD DEPENDED ON IT."

9. DISSOLVE TO TITLE WORD "NIXON." ZOOM INTO CU. HOLD. FADEOUT.

10. CLOSING NETWORK DISCLAIMER: "THE PRECEDING PRE-RECORDED POLITICAL BROADCAST WAS PAID FOR BY THE NIXON-AGNEW CAMPAIGN COMMITTEE."

E.S.J. #13
"BLACK CAPITALISM"

VIDEO	AUDIO
2. ESTABLISH MEAN-LOOK-ING GHETTO AREA.	R.N. The face of the ghetto is the face of despair.
3. BRIEF INDIVIDUAL SHOTS OF MEN, WOMEN, AND CHILDREN. THEY HAVE A WEARY LOOK ON THEIR FACES.	If we hope to light this face, we must rescue the ghetto from its despair.
4. LONG AND MEDIUM SHOTS OF SMALL CROWDS OF PEOPLE IN FRONT OF CLOSED STORES OR IN SITUA-TIONS WHERE THE MOOD IS ONE OF WAITING. THEY ARE POORLY DRESSED.	But not with more promises. Not with the old solution . . . the handout. We must offer a new so-lution . . . the hand-up.
5. ESTABLISHING SHOTS OF STORES OBVIOUSLY OWNED AND/OR RUN BY BLACK AMERICANS. A BUSY BANK—A CO-OP MARKET—A CLOTHING SHOP.	With your help, I will begin a new program to get private enter-prise into the ghetto and the ghetto into private enterprise. I call it "Black Capitalism."
6. MONTAGE OF ANIMATED FACES OF BUSY MEN AND WOMEN—ENTHUSIASTIC TEENAGERS, ETC. THE MOOD IS OF BUSY ACTIV-	MUSIC UP FULL.

VIDEO   AUDIO

ITY—BUYING, SELLING, WORKING.

7. MEDIUM SHOTS OF PEOPLE IN GROUPS WALKING ON STREETS. STOREFRONTS, LIGHTED, FILLED WITH PRODUCTS CAN BE SEEN. THERE IS A FEELING OF SUCCESS AND PROGRESS IN THE PHOTOS.

R.N.

More black ownership of business and land and homes can be the multiplier of pride that will end our racial strife.

8. SEVERAL SHOTS OF BLACK AND WHITE AMERICANS TOGETHER. THEY ARE TALKING, WALKING, WORKING. ON ONE WE DO A LONG PULLBACK AND FADE-OUT.

The black man's pride is the white man's hope.

TWO VERSIONS:
:60 seconds
:40 seconds

E.S.J. #15
"REACH OUT"

VIDEO   AUDIO

1. OPENING NETWORK DISCLAIMER: "A POLITICAL ANNOUNCEMENT."

2. FADEUP ON ZOOM INTO CROWD. NIXON IS SURROUNDED BY PEOPLE.

MUSIC UP FULL.

VIDEO	AUDIO
3. NIXON MOVES THROUGH CROWD, VARIOUS SHOTS FROM DIFFERENT PERSPECTIVES.	R.N. What has to be done, has to be done by the President and people together; or it won't be done at all.
4. MCU's OF ABOVE SEQUENCE.	I am asking not that you give something *to* your country, but that you do something *with* your country; I am asking not for your gifts, but for your hands.
5. WS NIXON AND CROWD SEPARATED BY ROOF OF CAR. ZOOM IN TO HANDS AS THEY REACH TOWARDS EACH OTHER.	
6. MONTAGE OF REACHING HANDS, SMILING FACES —NIXON AND PEOPLE. INCREASING TEMPO.	MUSIC UP FULL. MUSIC UNDER.
8. PULL BACK FROM CLASPED HANDS OF NIXON AND PEOPLE. TILT FROM PEOPLE IN WINDOW TO "NIXON FOR PRESIDENT" SIGN. PAN TO CU OF NIXON.	R.N. Together we can hardly fail, for there is no force on earth to match the will and spirit of the people of America.
9. ZOOM OUT FROM CU WORD "NIXON" TO REVEAL SIGN "NIXON'S THE ONE" ABOVE NIXON CAVALCADE SURROUNDED BY CHEERING THRONGS. HOLD. FADE-OUT.	MUSIC UP FULL. MUSIC OUT.

VIDEO   AUDIO

10. FADEUP TITLE: "THIS
    TIME VOTE LIKE YOUR
    WHOLE WORLD DE-
    PENDED ON IT."

11. DISSOLVE TO TITLE
    WORD "NIXON." ZOOM
    INTO CU. HOLD. FADE-
    OUT.

12. FADEUP ON NETWORK
    CLOSING DISCLAIMER:
    "THE PRECEDING PRE-
    RECORDED POLITICAL
    BROADCAST WAS PAID
    FOR BY THE NIXON-
    AGNEW CAMPAIGN COM-
    MITTEE."

                                    TWO VERSIONS:
                                    :60 seconds
                                    :40 seconds

                    E.S.J. #16
                    "WOMAN"

VIDEO   AUDIO
 1. OPENING NETWORK DIS-
    CLAIMER: "A POLITICAL
    ANNOUNCEMENT."

 2. FADEUP ON DIAGONAL   FADEUP WITH LOW BACK-
    VIEW DOWN ON SIDE-   GROUND SOUNDS OF THE
    WALK. IT IS A WET   CITY. SOUND OF CLICKING
    NIGHT. FEET OF WOMAN   HEELS.
    COME INTO VIEW.

VIDEO	AUDIO
3. SHE IS DRESSED IN A CLOTH COAT. LOOKS TO BE ABOUT AGE 45, APPARENTLY COMING HOME LATE FROM SHOPPING OR WORK. THE CAMERA BEGINS TO TRAVEL WITH HER.	ANNCR: Crimes of violence in the United States have almost doubled in recent years. Today a violent crime is committed every 60 seconds.
4. BEHIND HER MOVING FIGURE FLOWS BY THE METAL-GATE COVERING OF A LOCKED STOREFRONT. IT BEGINS TO GET DARKER AS WE MOVE IN FOR MCU WHILE TRAVELING WITH HER.	A robbery every 2½ minutes. A mugging every 6 minutes. A murder every 43 minutes.
5. MOVE IN TO CU FOR FINAL TRAVELING SEQUENCE.	And it will get worse unless we take the offensive.
6. WE ARE IN CLOSE-UP. CAMERA HOLDS. WOMAN WALKS OFF DOWN THE SIDEWALK. HOLD ON THIS VIEW AS HER FIGURE GROWS SMALLER AGAINST THE DARK NIGHT.	ANNCR: Freedom from fear is a basic right of every American. We must restore it. DISTANT HEEL CLICKS.
7. FADEOUT.	
8. FADEUP ON TITLE: "THIS TIME VOTE LIKE	

VIDEO   AUDIO

YOUR WHOLE WORLD
DEPENDED ON IT."

9. DISSOLVE   TO   TITLE
   WORD "NIXON." ZOOM
   INTO CU. HOLD. FADE-
   OUT.

10. CLOSING NETWORK DIS-
    CLAIMER: "THE PRECED-
    ING PRE-RECORDED PO-
    LITICAL   BROADCAST
    WAS PAID FOR BY THE
    NIXON-AGNEW   CAM-
    PAIGN COMMITTEE."